Allie Aller & Valerie Bothell

Quilting...

just a little bit crazy

A Marriage of Traditional & Crazy Quilting

10
Projects
· · · · · · · · · ·
30
Techniques

C&T PUBLISHING

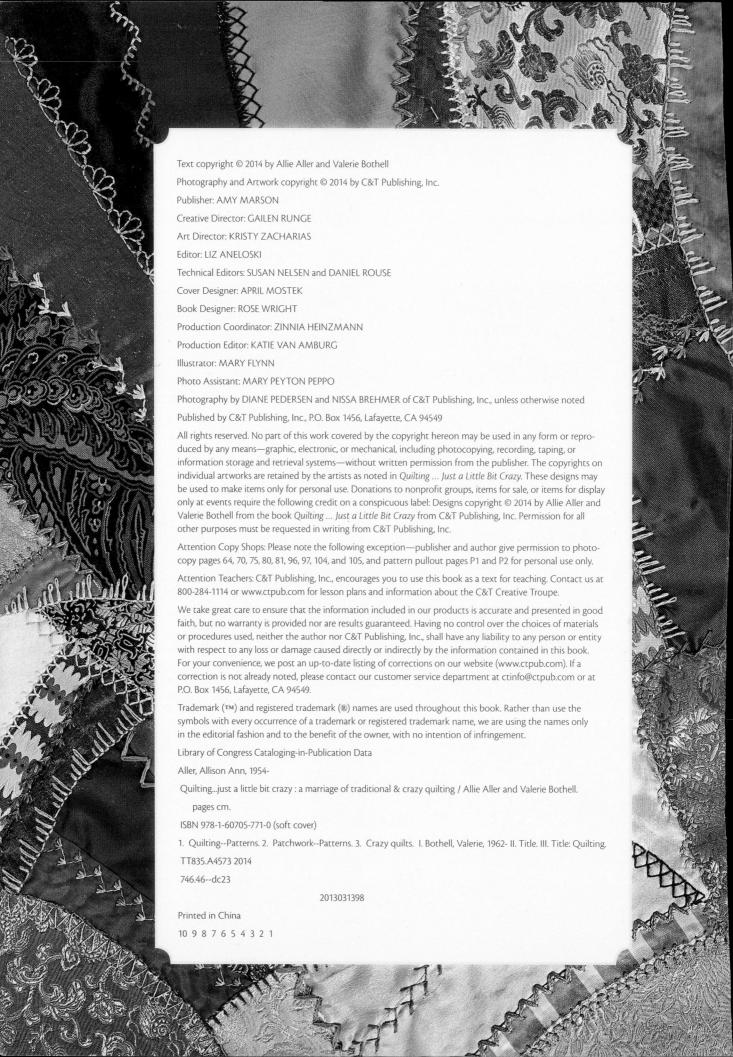

Text copyright © 2014 by Allie Aller and Valerie Bothell

Photography and Artwork copyright © 2014 by C&T Publishing, Inc.

Publisher: AMY MARSON

Creative Director: GAILEN RUNGE

Art Director: KRISTY ZACHARIAS

Editor: LIZ ANELOSKI

Technical Editors: SUSAN NELSEN and DANIEL ROUSE

Cover Designer: APRIL MOSTEK

Book Designer: ROSE WRIGHT

Production Coordinator: ZINNIA HEINZMANN

Production Editor: KATIE VAN AMBURG

Illustrator: MARY FLYNN

Photo Assistant: MARY PEYTON PEPPO

Photography by DIANE PEDERSEN and NISSA BREHMER of C&T Publishing, Inc., unless otherwise noted

Published by C&T Publishing, Inc., P.O. Box 1456, Lafayette, CA 94549

Library of Congress Cataloging-in-Publication Data

Aller, Allison Ann, 1954-

Quilting...just a little bit crazy : a marriage of traditional & crazy quilting / Allie Aller and Valerie Bothell.

    pages cm.

ISBN 978-1-60705-771-0 (soft cover)

1. Quilting--Patterns. 2. Patchwork--Patterns. 3. Crazy quilts. I. Bothell, Valerie, 1962- II. Title. III. Title: Quilting.

TT835.A4573 2014

746.46--dc23

                        2013031398

Printed in China

10 9 8 7 6 5 4 3 2 1

Dedication

Photo: Valerie Bothell

To Carole Samples, who brought us together.
We thank you and love you very much.

Acknowledgments

Allie I've been blessed with so many wonderful people who have lighted and smoothed the path this book has taken:

Thank you to Martha Green, Sharon Boggon, Carole Samples, and Judith Baker Montano, the "Big Four" in my crazy-quilt world over the last fifteen years, for leading the way into new ways of seeing and working. Meg Cox, Jodie Davis, Vicki Day, Brenda Groelz, Jean Krynicki, Mark Lipinski, Amy Milne, Edith Minne, Michele Muska, Linda Pumphrey, and Alex Veronelli have supplied me with friendship, encouragement, supplies, and tools to make my heart sing and to keep my hands busy. Seeing their professionalism in the quilt industry and serving with some of them on the board of the great nonprofit, the Quilt Alliance, has been a true inspiration to me. Tracey Brookshier, my quilt oracle, has always given me good advice. And thanks to Victoria Findlay Wolfe for her amazing *Fresh off the Farm* workingman's quilt, demonstrating how the modern quilt movement can go crazy too.

I especially want to thank my sister, Mary Landis, for her best friendship and always insightful, hilarious understanding; my husband, Robert, the center of my beautiful, crazy world; and most importantly, my co-author, Val. It has been an absolute joy working with you.

Val Over the years, many people have encouraged me on my crazy-quilt path. I would first like to thank my family for letting my crazy-quilt obsession take over several rooms in our house. For many years my children have watched their mommy "play with her ribbons."

Special thanks to Carole Samples for mentoring me when I didn't believe in myself, an act that means so much to me; to Judith Baker Montano for your friendship, advice, and encouragement; to my best friend, Dixie Derksen, for the support you have given me all of these years; to Jean Krynicki of River Silks for sending the most gorgeous box of silk ribbon I have ever seen; to Marin Hanson, curator of exhibitions at the International Quilt Study Center & Museum, for letting Allie and me look at *My Crazy Dream* to our heart's content; to all of my students who have come to my home over the last seventeen years and taken classes from me: It means so much to me that you thought I had something to offer you; to Victoria Findlay Wolfe for the use of her *Fresh off the Farm* workingman's quilt in our book; and to Allie, my co-author: It was a wonderful journey and I enjoyed every minute of it—you are the best. And to God, through whom all blessings flow …

Contents

Introduction   6

Crazy-Quilt Construction   7

Making Crazy-Quilt Blocks and Borders   7

Freezer-Paper Template Appliqué   7

Free-Form Appliqué   9

Cardstock Appliqué Crazy Piecing   11

Flip and Sew   13

Montano Piecing Methods   14

Crazy Piecing Long Borders   17

Assembling the Crazy-Quilt Top   18

Block Settings and Border Arrangements   18

Assembly Methods   20

Finishing Techniques   23

The Importance of Interfacing   23

How to Interface a Crazy-Quilt Top   23

Batting and Backing Choices   23

Fastening the Layers Together   24

Machine or Hand Quilting   24

Tied or Buttoned   24

Interior Tying Method   24

Piecing Directly onto Backing   26

Alternative Binding Techniques   28

Quilt Labels   31

Stitching and Embellishing   32

Hand Embroidery   32

Crazy-Quilt Stitches   33

Silk Ribbon Embroidery   39

Tips for Even Stitches   41

Embroidery Transfer   42

Hand Quilting   42

Machine Crazy-Quilt Embroidery ... Plus Some Handwork   43

Crazy-Quilt Machine Embroidery Stitching   43

The Projects

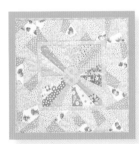

A Little Bit Crazy   52

Val   Crazy Bow Ties   52

Allie   Crazy for Plaid   59

Amish Wool Crazy   65

Val   Amish Bouquet   65

Allie   Ode to the Amish   71

Workingman's Crazy   76

Val   Fond Memories   76

Allie   Morning Chores   82

Fan-tastic Crazy   90

Val   Oriental Garden   90

Allie   Color Block Fans   98

Historically Crazy   106

Val   I Dream in Pink   107

Allie   My Washougal Dream   112

Resources   118

About the Authors   119

Introduction

Serendipity is responsible for the genesis of this book, a happy accident that became a most pleasant surprise. Val hosts the Victorian Stitchery Retreat every year in her hometown of Wichita, Kansas, and in 2011, both Allie and Carole Samples were teachers. Carole had asked if she could give a lecture that week, and Val was more than happy to say yes. The room was packed as everyone eagerly anticipated Carole's lecture. Just who do you think happened to sit together?

Carole gave the most moving lecture we have ever heard, bringing the Victorian crazy quilters of the 1880s so vividly to life that both of us were almost in tears, soaking in her passion for her subject. It turns out that we both shared a deep love for historical quilts, for Carole Samples and her legacy, and for our own work—giving those old quilts a new, modern life. The very next morning, we vowed to write a book together. Who would have ever thought that two girls from different states and different crazy-quilt styles would come together to write a book? … Serendipity!

The fruit of our labors is now in your hands. We want this book to serve you by combining both of our styles and offering you as many choices and techniques as we can, so crazy quilting will come alive for you too.

We hope it becomes a go-to resource for traditional as well as innovative crazy-quilting skills. You will find several ways to piece and appliqué crazy-quilt blocks and

wholecloth crazy quilts too. Val presents an extensive section with step-by-step photos of the basic crazy-quilt embroidery stitches, as well as a few basic silk ribbon stitches for the beginner. Allie explores combining machine embroidery with handwork in new ways, both to speed things up and to open up new possibilities for those who are not as enamored with handwork. We offer several techniques for finishing crazy quilts using unusual batting supplies, tying, or quilting, and we include unique binding strategies as well.

One of our major goals was to cross the quilting genre boundaries, to show that crazy quilts can be *functional*. We offer small, bed-size, and lap quilts, some of which incorporate lots of machine quilting. Truly, any traditional quilt can incorporate elements of crazy quilting, and any crazy quilt can include quilting … our aim is to show you how.

We each created our own version of each of the five themes presented. We hope to demonstrate how crazy quilting can reflect very different aesthetics and working methods. We also aim to show that you do not need a large stash, or even fancy fabrics, to make a crazy quilt. (There is a lot of cotton in evidence here.) While Allie's projects reflect decades of collecting fabrics, Val's fabrics were purchased specifically for her projects. Either approach works great and yields a lovely quilt.

It is our final hope that you find as much joy in creating these projects as we have.

Val and Allie

Crazy-Quilt Construction

In this chapter we present many techniques for constructing blocks and for assembling and finishing crazy quilts. We have each distilled our combined experience of 30 years in crazy quilting, so you can jump right in with the method and style that works best for you.

Sometimes we will sew blocks and borders together, as with any traditional quilt top. But more often, we appliqué fabrics and even blocks onto a foundation. (To appliqué is to *apply* a layer of fabric on top of another, with a finished or a raw edge.) We offer both hand and machine techniques for appliqué, all of which yield a block ready for embellishment.

Making Crazy-Quilt Blocks and Borders

Allie Freezer-Paper Template Appliqué

Sewing a block using freezer-paper templates traced from patterns ensures that you will be able to exactly replicate that block's design. Believe it or not, this is sometimes desirable in crazy quilting. Randomness and repetition can be a great combination when designing these quilts.

This is also a fabulous technique for achieving perfectly controlled curved patches in crazy quilts, with easy sewing and little fuss. The only tools you need are an iron, plenty of sharp pins, and a machine with a zigzag stitch. The necessary supplies are simple, too: freezer and tracing papers, fabric and paper markers, muslin and interfacing for the foundation, fabric scraps, and some clear thread for the top with machine-weight sewing thread for the bobbin. See Pain-Free Sewing with Invisible Thread (page 10). A lightbox is helpful, but you can always use a bright window for tracing the block diagram onto the freezer paper.

Let's go through the process together.

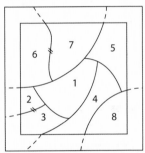

Ode to the Amish block

Before we begin, please notice three things on the block diagram (above).

1. The inner perimeter line shows *the finished sewn edges* of this block, at 6″ × 6″. The patches are measured and cut out with a margin on all perimeter edges—the outer line—to allow for plenty of room when trimming the blocks to size. So, although the block is cut out at 7¾″ × 7¾″, it will be trimmed to 6½″ × 6½″ and will finish at 6″ × 6″.

2. The patch shapes are numbered in the sequence in which they will be appliquéd onto the muslin.

3. The crosshatch marks between patches 2 and 3 and patches 6 and 7 denote that these pairs are appliquéd together first, along their common edges, before they are appliquéd as a single unit onto the muslin.

 Note

One pattern can be varied by tracing it backwards. The resulting blocks are visually related, yet interestingly different. And they will still look "crazy." To use this technique, trace the block pattern onto tracing paper. Then flip the tracing paper and trace those lines onto freezer paper. Refer to Preparing the Foundations and Templates, Steps 1 and 2 (page 72), to see a pattern and its reversed image with the markings.

PREPARING THE FOUNDATION AND FABRIC PATCHES

1. Refer to the Ode to the Amish block pattern (page 75). Trace the block diagram onto paper. Use a marker for a heavy line.

2. Cut freezer paper, muslin, and interfacing into 7¾″ × 7¾″ squares.

3. Trace the block design onto the dull side of the freezer paper with a marker. Number the patches and include the crosshatch marks.

4. Next, lightly trace the block design onto the muslin using a pencil. These lines are to help you position the patches; you don't need to include the numbers.

5. Fuse the interfacing to the back of the traced muslin square.

6. Cut apart the freezer-paper templates on the lines.

7. Iron the shiny side of freezer-paper patch 1 to the *right* side of the first fabric. Draw around the template using a pencil, chalk line, or anything that will show up well but is still removable. Chalk is particularly good on wool.

Iron patch 1 onto fabric and mark around template.

8. Remove the freezer-paper template and set aside for reuse. Cut out the shape, leaving a healthy ¼″ margin around the drawn line. You do not have to measure this; just eyeball it.

9. Repeat for all 8 patches.

10. Sew patches 2 and 3 together along their common seam, using the marked lines to help you align them properly. Repeat for patches 6 and 7.

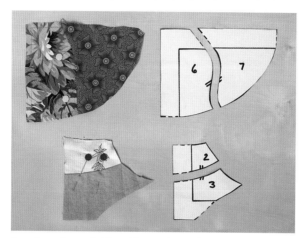

Sew pieces for patch 2/3 and for patch 6/7 along their common edges.

Tips

● **Store freezer-paper templates in a plastic bag to help keep track of them. You'll be able to reuse them several times.**

● **Arrange prepared fabric patches in place on top of the block diagram drawing. As you sew, you'll easily find the patch you need.**

APPLIQUÉING THE BLOCK

1. Pin patch 1 in place on the muslin.

2. Fold ¼″ under and iron the edge on patch 2/3 that overlaps patch 1, along the marked line. Pin into place, over patch 1, using the marked line for placement.

3. Fold ¼″ under and iron the edge on patch 4 that overlaps patches 1 and 2/3. Pin it into place.

4. Repeat with patches 5, 6/7, and 8.

Pinning patches in place

5. Once the block is all pinned, machine appliqué all the patches using a clear top thread and machine thread in the bobbin. Refer to Pain-Free Sewing with Invisible Thread (page 10).

6. Press the block from the back.

7. With a removable marker, mark the finished sewing line on the block, and then trim the edges ¼" beyond the sewing line, making the block 6½" × 6½". As a very important last step, straight stitch or zigzag around the perimeter of the block to stabilize the edges.

Sewing line of block marked with removable marker. (Seam allowances shown are extra wide for illustration purposes.) Note that this is the block design used in Allie's *Ode to the Amish* (page 71).

Allie Free-Form Appliqué

I love the spontaneity of this way of working. Patches are cut out freely and their edges ironed under. Then they're pinned, overlapping each other—just as in Freezer-Paper Template Appliqué (page 7), but without templates. I've used this method in half of my projects in this book.

You'll need the same tools and supplies as in Freezer-Paper Template Appliqué—except, since there is no pattern, there is no tracing or marking, so skip the papers and pens.

For an example, I will demonstrate this technique using a 4" × 11" border foundation strip (1" larger than the required unfinished border strip).

1. Cut and fuse together a piece of interfacing and a piece of muslin.

2. Place the first patch onto the muslin. Cut more patches, turning under and ironing the straight edges that will overlap, pinning them into place as you go.

3. Cut a patch with a curve along its adjoining edge, and pin alongside the others. Do not turn under and iron this edge, but leave it raw.

4. Cover the raw-edge curve with trim, and pin it into place. Pieces can be pinned into place before the shape is completely cut out, as shown in the photo.

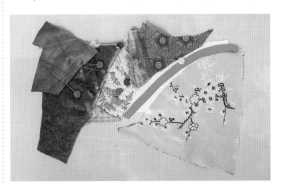

Border strip under construction

5. Continue this process until the entire muslin foundation is covered with pinned patches and trim.

6. Appliqué with a zigzag stitch, using a clear top thread and machine thread in the bobbin.

7. Iron the strip from the back. Trim the piece to size (3" × 10" for the border strip in my example) and secure the perimeter edge with stitching.

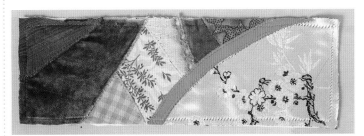

Completed border strip

I encourage you to practice this method to get a feel for it. It's fun and easy. Of course, you can always appliqué free-form patches by hand as well. It just depends on how you like to work.

Tips

● Inserting lace or trim under a folded edge during the pinning process (before sewing) is an easy way to add interest to a block with almost no extra work.

● Because trim has finished edges along each side, it can be appliquéd right over the raw edge of a fabric patch, with no need to turn the edge under and iron it as long as the raw ends of the trim go into a seam allowance. Using trim this way can be especially helpful with fabrics that can melt if ironed and with heavy fabrics that would be too thick to lie flat with the edge folded under.

● Trim can be ironed into a curved shape to match a curve between patches. To do this, hold one end of the trim and pull it toward you as you iron the trim away from you and to the side. This motion sets a nice gentle arc into the trim, as is shown in the completed border strip photo (page 9).

● You can lay out a free-form appliqué block to feature a special fabric motif, as in the example at right.

Free-form appliqué block featuring floral motif in center, shown here in three stages of completion with sewing line marked with removable marker

Pain-Free Sewing with Invisible Thread

● Monofilament clear thread is stretchy, so the upper tension on the machine must be loosened quite a bit. (Make sure the presser foot is down while you adjust the tension.) Use an interfaced sample cloth to test the stitching as you gradually loosen the upper tension, until you get a smooth stitch with no puckers and no bobbin thread showing between the top stitches.

● A 50-weight bobbin thread is best, but any machine thread can be used. Choose a neutral color or one that matches the color scheme of the work.

● Use a topstitching machine needle. The large eye makes a huge difference.

● Monofilament thread unspools easily. A netted thread sleeve over the spool can help provide a little extra tension to the thread as it comes off the spool. You could also try tying a piece of yarn around the spool, with the thread feeding out toward the top.

● Use a permanent marker to dot the end of the thread, making it easier to see when threading the needle.

● Sew slowly. Fast starts, especially, can jerk the spool and cause the thread to unwind too fast.

● Throughout this book, I have set my zigzag stitch at 2.5mm wide and 1.5mm long in all my invisible thread sewing. You'll have to experiment to find the best settings for your machine.

● My brands of choice:

YLI Wonder Invisible Thread is a nylon thread. It is cross-wound on the spool, so it benefits from an upright spool pin.

Superior MonoPoly Thread is polyester. It is wound parallel on the spool, so it works best with a horizontal spool pin. Some say polyester thread is less "glinty" than nylon.

Val Cardstock Appliqué Crazy Piecing

Several years ago, I became interested in introducing curves and different-sized shapes into my crazy quilting. I played around with different ideas that would help me to achieve the finished look I wanted. I had cardstock on hand because I have used it for many years to make templates for my stitching on the blocks. It occurred to me that cardstock could also be used to help me piece blocks!

You can purchase 8½" × 11" cardstock from any hobby or office supply store. For this method I do not recommend velvets or heavy polyester fabrics that will not press well. You can always experiment with the fabric, and if the ones you have chosen don't work, just try something else. The numbers on the block indicate the piecing order. The hash marks on the pattern indicate pieces that will be sewn together before they are pieced onto the muslin foundation. This method uses both machine sewing and hand appliqué to piece the block.

1. Photocopy Allie's block pattern Ode to the Amish in Freezer-Paper Template Appliqué (page 7) onto cardstock. This will be a 6" finished block.

2. Cut a piece of muslin ½" larger than the block. Lay the muslin on top of the cardstock copy, and trace the pattern onto the muslin using a fine-tip permanent marker. (I use a Sharpie.) Numbers and crosshatch marks are not needed on the muslin.

3. Number the cardstock pattern pieces and cut the pattern apart to make the templates.

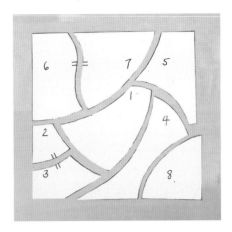

Tip

Because you have cut the pattern into pieces, it is a good idea to have an extra copy of the pattern for reference. It's just like having a picture of a puzzle so you know how to put it back together!

4. Place template 1, number side down, on the wrong side of the fabric. Trace the template (I use an air-erasable pen) and cut out, leaving a generous ¼" seam allowance all the way around the shape.

5. Pin fabric piece 1 in place on the muslin block, right side up.

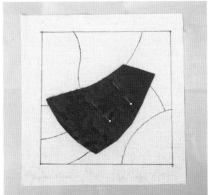

6. Trace fabric pieces 2 and 3, laying the templates, number side down, on the wrong side of the fabric. Cut out as in Step 4.

7. Machine stitch pieces 2 and 3, right sides together, with a ¼" seam allowance. Refer to the original pattern to make sure you are sewing the correct 2 sides together. The seam is a bit curved, so ease the fabric along as you sew. Trim the seam to ⅛" and press.

8. Lay this sewn unit wrong side up, and place the templates, number sides down, on the wrong side of the fabric. Pressing only the edge shown, press under ¼" to prepare the edge to hand appliqué to fabric piece 1.

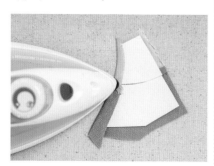

9. Lay templates 2 and 3 in position on the muslin block as shown. Using a marker, mark along the edge that adjoins fabric piece 1, so you will know where to place the fabric unit in the next step.

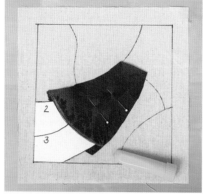

Tip

You can use any marking pencil to do this. I prefer to use a purple air-erasable pen most of the time. If the fabric is dark, I use a chalk pencil or chalk marker. Use a water-erasable pen only if the fabrics you are using can get wet.

10. Lay fabric unit 2/3 along the marked line, pin in place, and hand appliqué it to the foundation using a blind hem stitch. Trim the seam allowance underneath, if needed.

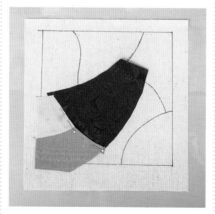

11. Lay template 4, number side down, on the wrong side of the fabric and cut out. Press under ¼" on the edge that will adjoin fabric piece 1.

12. Lay template 4 in place on the muslin block and mark a line so you will know where to place fabric piece 4. Lay fabric piece 4 along the marked line, pin in place, and appliqué to the foundation. Trim the seam, if needed.

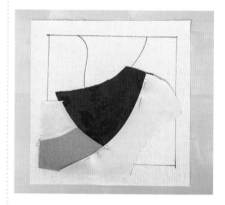

13. Continue, adding piece 5.

14. Cut out the fabric shapes for pieces 6 and 7. I found this curved seam to be too curvy to sew on my machine, so I appliquéd the 2 pieces together by hand.

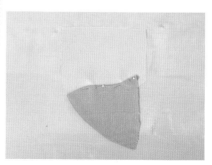

15. Iron under the curved edge that will adjoin fabric piece 1, mark the placement line, pin, and machine appliqué into place.

16. Continue, adding piece 8.

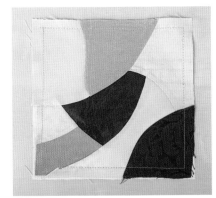

Finished block

Tip

After I am done piecing, I always turn the block upside down and press it. Then I sew ⅛˝ around the edge of the block so it doesn't fray.

Enjoy embellishing your new block!

Val Flip and Sew

1. Copy the Thrifty Housewife pattern B (page 81) onto paper. Lay a pattern-size piece of muslin (or you can use a piece of an old sheet as the foundation for this block) on top of the copy and trace the block using a fine-tip permanent marker.

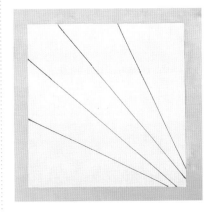

2. Cut a piece of fabric large enough to fit in the bottom wedge. Make the piece large enough to extend over the muslin edges and the marker line by at least ¼˝. Lay the fabric right side up on the bottom wedge.

3. Cut a piece of fabric large enough to fit in the second wedge, adding at least an extra ¼˝ for seam allowances all the way around. Lay it wrong side down on the first piece of fabric, matching up the edges as shown, and pin into place.

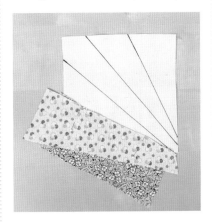

4. Flip the block over to the wrong side and sew on the first marker line on the left. Flip the block back over to the right side. Trim the seam, fold the second piece of fabric open to the right side, and press.

5. Repeat Steps 3 and 4 to finish the block.

6. Turn the block to the wrong side and press well. Trim away any extra fabric that extends past the outside edge of the muslin square, and stitch a ⅛˝ basting stitch all the way around the block.

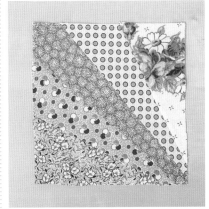

Montano Piecing Methods

In 1986, Judith Baker Montano brought new life to the crazy-quilting world with her book *The Crazy Quilt Handbook*. In this book, she introduced two styles of piecing blocks that are very effective in achieving a beautiful crazy quilt. I have chosen to simplify these foundation-piecing methods to achieve the desired effect for each of the projects that utilize her methods. Foundation piecing essentially means that you will be sewing different pieces of fabric to a muslin base. The muslin foundation can be any size or shape. These methods use machine stitching.

If you are a beginner, make a practice block before starting any of the projects; I find an 8″ square to be a good beginning size.

MONTANO CENTERPIECE METHOD

1. Cut a 5-sided fabric shape and pin it, right side up, in the center of a square piece of muslin.

2. Cut a rectangular piece that will fit on a side of the center fabric.

3. Pin the rectangular piece, wrong side up, aligning it with the straight edge, and sew with a ⅛″ seam allowance. Press open.

4. *Working clockwise*, cut the next piece of fabric. It should be long enough to cover the rectangular piece of fabric and the next side of the 5-sided shape.

5. Pin the piece, wrong side up, and sew a ⅛″ seam allowance. Trim the seam and press open.

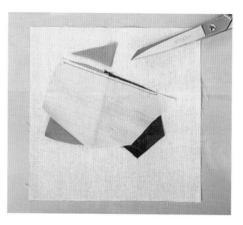

 Tip

To make the block more interesting, start cutting different shapes of fabric other than the rectangular shape you started with.

6. Continue this process for the third, fourth, and fifth sides of the 5-sided shape.

7. Continue working clockwise until the muslin is completely covered. Trim the outside edges even with the muslin square. Sew around the perimeter of the block ⅛" from the edge. This will keep the outer edges of the fabric in place.

✦ *Tip*

You can give a block a "crazier" look by sewing two pieces of fabric together and then treating them as one piece when you sew them in place.

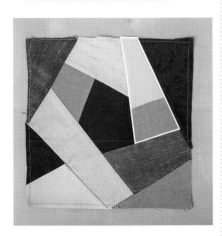

✦ *Tip*

It is always a good idea to repeat some of the fabrics you have used in a block a couple of times. Strategically place them so the block looks balanced.

Montano Fan Method

1. Cut a 5-sided fabric shape with a 90° corner and pin it, right side up, to the lower left corner of a square piece of muslin.

2. *Working clockwise,* cut a rectangular piece that will fit on the top left raw edge of the 5-sided shape. Pin the rectangular piece, wrong side up, aligned with the straight edge of the 5-sided shape, and sew a ⅛" seam allowance. Press open.

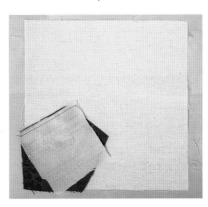

✦ *Tip*

To make the block more interesting, start cutting different shapes of fabric other than the rectangular shape you started with.

3. Cut a third piece of fabric. It should be long enough to cover the previous rectangular piece of fabric and align with the next side of the 5-sided shape. Some of the rectangle will extend beyond this new piece and will be trimmed later. Pin the piece, wrong side up, and sew a ⅛" seam allowance. Now trim the seam of the previous piece and press open.

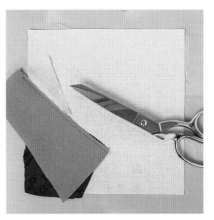

4. Cut a fourth piece of fabric long enough to cover the right edge of the very first corner piece. Pin into place on the right edge and sew a ⅛" seam allowance. Trim the seam and press open.

5. Now working counterclockwise, cut a piece of fabric to cover part of the right edge of the piece you attached in Step 4. Pin in place and sew a ⅛″ seam allowance. Trim the seam and press open.

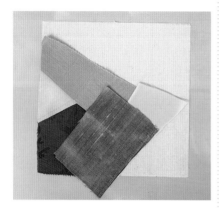

6. Cut another piece of fabric, long enough to cover the right edges of the last 2 pieces that you added. Pin in place and sew a ⅛″ seam allowance. Trim the seam and press open.

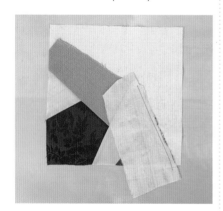

7. Continue piecing the block counterclockwise until you reach the left edge of the muslin square. When you have reached the edge, begin to work *clockwise* until you have covered the muslin.

8. Trim the outside edges even with the muslin square and sew around the perimeter of the block ⅛″ from the edge.

✦ *Tip*

You can give a block a "crazier" look by sewing two pieces of fabric together and then treating them as one piece when you sew them in place.

Val Crazy Piecing Long Borders

For *Fond Memories* (page 76), I modified the Montano Centerpiece Method (page 14) to make long crazy-pieced borders for a modern look. This method uses machine stitching.

1. Cut the border according to project instructions and, starting in the middle, begin piecing using the Montano Centerpiece Method.

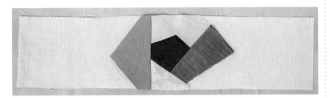

2. Cut various sizes of near-rectangular shapes with unusual angles and begin to build the pieced border by stitching them in place.

> **Tip**
>
> The next few steps will help break up the long, near-rectangular pieces that are beginning to appear. The border will have a "crazier" look with more pieces in the mix.

3. Cut 2 rectangular shapes of fabric and sew them together. Press the seam open.

4. Sew the pieced unit to the next available raw edge to the right.

5. Cut a triangular piece of fabric and sew it in place. This will help to create even more unusual angles on the border.

6. Continue using the methods in Steps 2–5 to create a finished border. Vary the techniques throughout the length of the border to achieve a "crazy" look to the piece.

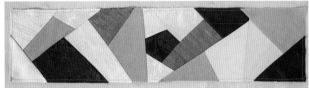

> **Tip**
>
> If you look closely at the fabrics in the finished example border, you will see that I balanced the placement of the colors fairly evenly from end to end to create a balanced block that is appealing to the eye.

Assembling the Crazy-Quilt Top

Block Settings and Border Arrangements

Once you have a beautiful pile of blocks and borders, how will you use them in a crazy quilt?

Allie has long been fascinated by the idea of creating hybrid quilts that combine both crazy and traditional ("sane") quilt techniques and aesthetics. As always in quilting, there are both technical and design decisions to make in this endeavor.

The main design consideration is how to set, or arrange, the crazy blocks and borders you have made. There are so many options! Using the same set of blocks and borders with a cream quilted background, here are a few of the many different looks you can achieve.

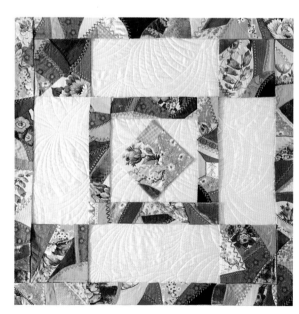

You can easily increase the design possibilities by adding trim, which can function as either a narrow border or sashing. Using trim gives you the option of covering the raw edges of blocks and border strips, rather than turning them under, when you are appliquéing them onto a foundation. Trim can enrich a quilt by adding a lot of interest.

Assembly Methods

There are several ways to assemble any quilt top. The most conventional method is to sew the blocks together, or sew blocks and sashing strips together, add borders, and so forth. Another way is to have a wholecloth foundation, the size of the entire quilt, and to appliqué the blocks, sashing, and border strips onto it. This foundation may be entirely covered or used as a background for the blocks so that some of it shows as part of the quilt's design, as in *Color Block Fans* (page 98). Or you can combine both methods: Sew together a row of blocks and then appliqué the row onto a foundation, as in *Morning Chores* (page 82).

Keeping some tips in mind will help you be successful with either approach.

TIPS FOR ASSEMBLY ON A FOUNDATION

- Interfacing the foundation fabric helps keep it from wobbling under the weight of the appliquéd blocks. Whether used on muslin strips for a long, wide border, as in *Morning Chores* (page 82), or on a large piece of silk velvet, as in *Color Block Fans* (page 98), interfacing gives a stable surface for appliquéing onto a foundation.

- To create finished edges so you can appliqué the blocks, fold under and iron edges along the finished seamline. Hold the seam allowances in place with a strip of Steam-A-Seam fusible tape slipped under the folded edge and fused.

- If you use wide ribbon for sashing, it is a good idea to interface the ribbon. You can cut interfacing strips to the proper width with a rotary cutter and ruler, cut them with a die cutting machine like the AccuQuilt, or mark them with a ruler and cut with scissors. You can also

Interfacing used to stabilize 1½″ acetate plaid ribbon

buy precut rolls of interfacing, such as Make It Simpler Fusible Interfacing (C&T Publishing).

- One way to integrate some machine quilting into a crazy quilt is to machine quilt the background fabric before appliquéing the blocks and borders. Or you can appliqué first and quilt second.

- It is a good idea to add embroidery and embellishment to the blocks and borders before you appliqué them to any foundation, though you can add more after the top is all together, if you just have to!

TIPS FOR ASSEMBLY WITH SEAMS

- In order to reduce bulk, press the seams between blocks and borders open. To keep the pressed-open seams flat, the gifted crazy-quilt artist Sharon Boggon uses a herringbone stitch along each seam allowance, lightly securing it to the back of the block. Now that is commitment!

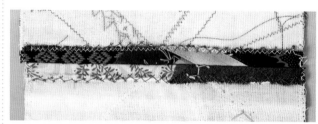

Use a herringbone stitch to hold seams open.

- If you are sashing the embellished blocks with single-layer fabric strips, use *two or even three* layers of interfacing on the strips. You want them to be the same weight as the blocks, or the quilt will not lie or hang flat, and the blocks won't be adequately supported.

- Instead of sewing blocks and borders together with seams, you can also "join" them with a strip of trim appliquéd onto the foundation, as in *Color Block Fans* (page 98). Always use a ruler to make sure the trim is parallel to the borders and blocks as you pin the layers together before appliquéing.

The Cowgirl's CQ by Allison Aller, 66" × 72", 2012.
Allie used interfaced and appliquéd trim to join the border strips together while assembling this quilt top.

The Cowgirl's CQ, detail

Finishing Techniques

Crazy quilts are usually made to be decorative, but in this book we are presenting many functional ones, too. You can tie, sew buttons, or quilt to hold the layers together. Batting, backing, and binding can enhance a quilt's functionality and the choices you make can speed up the sewing process, too. Whether you want an elegant finish for a wallhanging, or a cozy and sturdy quilt to use over the years on the couch or bed, you will find ideas here that really *work*.

The Importance of Interfacing

Interfacing is used on muslin foundations, fabric sashing strips, wiggly velvet or silk, and wide ribbon used as sashing. But there is another place to use it, specifically on heavily embellished crazy quilts meant for the wall.

Once you have sewn blocks and borders together to create a quilt top, it is amazingly helpful to interface the entire crazy-quilt top from the back. One continuous layer across the assembled blocks melds the top into a whole. Without being stiff, it hangs straight and even, like a single piece of cloth.

How to Interface a Crazy-Quilt Top

This is how we interface a quilt top, but it's always a good idea to read the manufacturer's instructions for the interfacing brand you use.

1. Lay some terry cloth bath towels over the ironing surface, whether it's a table or the floor.

2. Spread the crazy-quilt top face down on the towels and smooth out any wrinkles.

3. Lay a single layer of fusible knit interfacing over the back of the quilt top, glue side down (the glue side is slightly rough to the touch). Although 60″-wide fusible knit interfacing is available, you can easily use the narrower width that is more commonly sold. Just overlap the edges by an inch or 2.

4. Turn off the steam and set the iron to medium-high. Place a piece of tracing paper or parchment paper between the iron and the interfacing. Starting at the center of the quilt top, gently press down onto the quilt and slowly fuse the interfacing, ironing away from the center and toward an outer edge of the quilt. Before you press it with the iron, smooth out any wrinkles in the interfacing as you go. Then go back to the center and iron out toward the other edges, an edge at a time.

5. Trim off any excess interfacing.

Batting and Backing Choices

A quilt's function will determine the batting and backing you choose. Here are some unusual ideas:

- Cotton drapery lining: This woven cloth is somewhat thicker than flannel but has a looser weave. It provides an excellent flat and structured batting for the inside of a decorative crazy quilt and causes no puffiness when the quilt sandwich is either tied or quilted. It is Allie's batting of choice. Find it in the home decorating section of the fabric store.

- Flannel sheet: *Fond Memories* (page 76) and *Morning Chores* (page 82) both use upcycled flannel sheets for the batting layer. The quilts are surprisingly warm and sturdy, especially with their lightweight denim backings.

- Microfiber plush (such as minky or cuddle fabric): Use minky as a combined backing/batting, so the quilts are made of two layers, not three. Crazy-quilt tops made from all-cotton fabrics with a plush backing/batting make for an especially soft and cuddly quilt.

- Polar fleece: A crazy-quilt top quilted directly onto polar fleece yields a wonderful bedspread! Simply pin baste the top to the polar fleece and machine quilt the two layers together. *The Cowgirl's CQ* (page 21) was done this way.

Fastening the Layers Together

Here are four different methods to hold batting, backing, and quilt top together:

Machine or Hand Quilting

BY MACHINE

If a crazy quilt does not have any beadwork or three-dimensional embellishment, it can be machine quilted just like any other quilt. Quilting lines can go right over the seam embroidery if necessary. However, it seems preferable to quilt in open areas between blocks. Take a look at the quilts in Amish Wool Crazy (page 65) and Fan-tastic Crazy (page 90). Or a quilt can be simply stitched in-the-ditch between its main sections, as in Morning Chores (page 82).

You have put so much time into your lovely crazy quilt, so do finish it properly. Using a self-threading needle, bring each quilting thread tail to the back and tie it off with its bobbin thread. Rethread both knotted tails again in the self-threading needle, and take a ½" stitch under the backing fabric before bringing the threads to the surface of the back again. Clip them off at the surface.

The quilting will never pull out over time, and the front and back will be perfectly neat, always. Allie thanks David Taylor for showing her this technique.

BY HAND

The borders on I Dream in Pink (page 107) were filled with decorative hand quilting using a silk thread (YLI button-hole twist) and a size 22 chenille needle. Not only does the quilting give the quilt a little more stability, but it also adds some character.

Tied or Buttoned

TIED

Traditionally, crazy quilts were tied and knotted with short threads or yarns that passed through all the quilt's layers at evenly spaced intervals, with the ties on the front or back of the quilt. This is still a viable option, with the ties adding a design element; 4mm silk ribbon is a great choice for tying a crazy quilt in this manner.

BUTTONED

A button provides more surface area than a single knot. Therefore, to sew through a button on the back of the quilt to the front and then back into the button again several times gives more support at the point of fastening. You can also use pairs of buttons, on the back and the front, sewing them together through the quilt layers, as is done in Crazy for Plaid (page 59). This takes a little longer, but it adds some very nice design possibilities, since the buttons are not only functional but decorative as well.

 Val Interior Tying Method

Most crazy quilts are made with heavy fabrics that are hard to quilt through, so I usually "inside tie" them. It is a great way to stabilize a crazy quilt and attach it to the backing fabric with no ties showing on the front.

There is always the choice of whether to put batting in the interior of a crazy quilt. If the quilt is fairly large I don't want the extra weight of batting, but when the project is small, batting helps give the quilt more shape. These instructions show you how to inside tie with batting in the interior of the crazy quilt. To further stabilize a crazy quilt, you could use this method in conjunction with interfacing. See How to Interface a Crazy-Quilt Top (page 23). Perle cotton size 8 is a good thread for smaller projects; size 5 is heavier and works well for larger projects. A size 22 chenille needle is just the right size for stitching through thick seam allowances.

1. Cut the backing fabric 1½"–2" larger than the finished quilt, and cut the batting to fit the finished size of the crazy-quilt top. Lay the backing fabric out, wrong side up. Place the batting in the center of the backing fabric and the finished crazy quilt on top of the batting, right side up.

> ### Note
> With the backing fabric 1½"–2" larger than the quilt top, you can use the method in Fold-Over Binding (page 28). If you want to use a different binding option, check the instructions for that method for guidance in cutting the backing.

2. Smooth out the crazy quilt and then baste down the middle of the quilt, through all the layers, with safety pins.

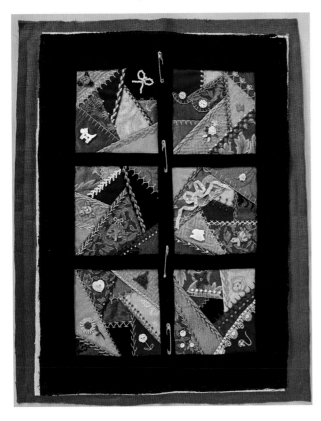

> ### Tip
>
> You can use quilt basting spray in place of safety pins. Just spray the section of the crazy-quilt top you want to pin and smooth into place on top of the batting. It is a little faster than safety pins if you are in a hurry.

3. Flip the right-hand side of the crazy quilt open all the way to the safety pins, as if you are turning a page in a book.

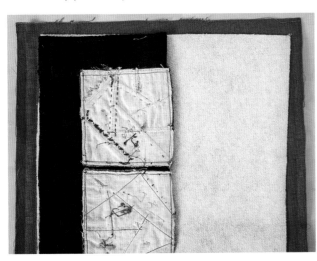

4. Take the threaded chenille needle and stitch down through the batting and backing near a seam allowance of the quilt top. Bring the needle back up, catching the seam allowance. Leave enough thread on each side of the stitch to tie a knot.

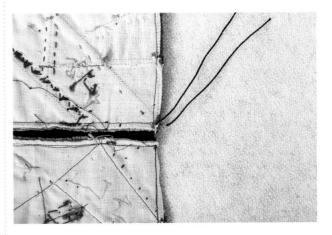

5. Tie a tight, firm knot 3 times and then clip the thread, leaving a ¾″ tail. The stitch on the back should not be very big.

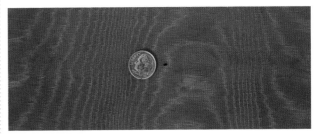

Small stitch on back

> ### Tip
>
> I usually tie at each corner of each crazy-quilt block. If the blocks are big, I also tie every 8″ to 10″ between the corners.

6. Move the crazy-quilt top back in place, so the right side is showing again. Smooth the quilt out, working from the center and moving outward. Move the safety pins over 8″ to 10″ and pin all the way down the quilt again. If you are using basting spray, just spray the next 8″ to 10″ of the quilt top and smooth into place.

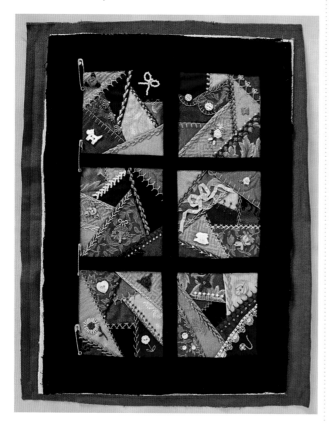

7. Continue working out from the center until you have tied the entire crazy quilt.

Val Piecing Directly onto Backing

Another great way to attach a quilt with sashing to the background fabric (such as polar fleece, minky, or denim) is to piece it directly to the backing as I did in *Crazy Bow Ties* (page 52). I layered denim with a thin flannel batting and treated these backing/batting layers as one unit. I also used this method for *Fond Memories* (page 76). I enjoyed the process, and it was a quick way to finish a quilt with no additional quilting required.

Note
Specific instructions for piecing order and block placement are found in project instructions for the quilts that use this method.

1. Lay the background fabric (or the background/batting unit) wrong side up and place the pieced block, right side up, on top of the backing in the appropriate position. Pin the sashing piece to a side of the block, wrong side up.

2. Sew a ¼″ seam allowance through all the layers. Press open. Pin the outside edge of the sashing through all layers, making sure the background fabric is smoothed out.

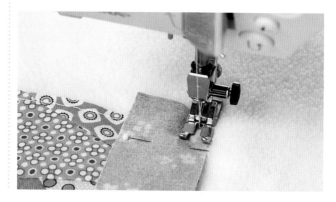

3. Continue working around the square clockwise, working in the same manner until you have done all the sashing. Trim excess pieces of fabric as needed.

 Tip

As I am working my way around a square or rectangle, I like to double-check that everything is squared up. When I position the piece that is going to be stitched in place next, I double-check by laying a clear grid ruler on top of it, lining the piece up with a 90° angle. I adjust as needed to make sure the piece is square and pin into place through all layers.

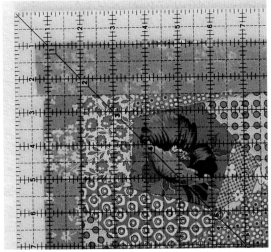

Square up as you go.

First round of sashing completed

4. Pin the next piece that is to be stitched to the sashing, wrong side up, through all the layers, making sure it is squared up. Sew a ¼" seam allowance and trim the excess pieces of fabric. Press open. Pin the outside edge of the strip.

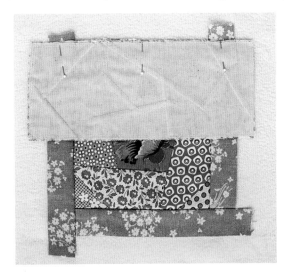

5. Continue working around the block clockwise, repeating Steps 1–4.

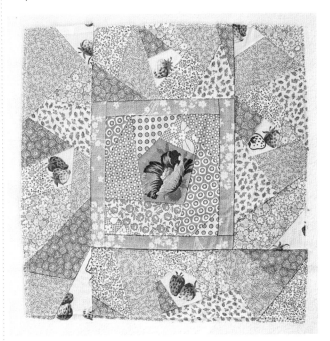

Alternative Binding Techniques

You can use your favorite traditional binding methods or try some of Allie's more unusual ones. Just remember that functionality and support of the quilt's design should always be what determines your choice of finishing technique.

FOLD-OVER BINDING

This method is used on *Ode to the Amish* (page 71). Functional and simple, the folded edge adds no design element to the quilt.

To create a fold-over binding, first layer the backing, batting, and quilt top. Cut the batting even with the quilt top. Then, to determine how much to trim the backing, decide on the width of binding that you want to show on the quilt front. Multiply that width by 2, and cut the backing that much larger on each side. Here's an example:

1. For a ½″ binding on the quilt front, multiply ½″ × 2 = 1″, so cut the backing fabric 1″ larger on each side than the quilt top and batting (if you are using batting). For this example, if the quilt top is 36″ × 36″, then cut the backing 38″ × 38″.

2. Fold in the backing edge ½″ so the raw edge of the backing meets the raw edge of the quilt top. Press.

3. Fold the backing fabric again, so it extends ½″ onto the right side of the quilt top. Pin in place. Use extra pins at the corners to make sure the folded edges make a 90° angle. Use a ruler to check, and adjust the pinning if necessary.

4. Machine appliqué the folded edge, using clear thread in the top and bobbin thread that matches the quilt backing fabric. Remove the pins so you don't sew over them.

FOLDED-IN-AND-STITCHED EDGE

Morning Chores (page 82) is an example of this binding method. The embroidered narrow outer border strips act as visual binding, without the work.

1. Trim the quilt sandwich ½″ beyond the final finished edge.

2. Fold the raw edges of the top and batting layers ½″ toward the center of the quilt sandwich and press, all the way around the quilt.

3. Fold in the raw edges of the backing layer ½″ toward the center of the quilt sandwich, aligning them evenly with the folded top and batting layers. Press and pin the layers together as you make your way around the quilt.

4. Stitch the folds closed, either by hand with a whipstitch, or by machine in a zigzag stitch with clear thread in the top and machine thread in the bobbin that matches the quilt backing fabric.

TRIM BINDING

Folding wide (at least 1″) lace, rickrack, or other trim to cover the edge of a quilt is especially quick because the trim's edges are already finished and need no folding under.

1. After quilting, cut all the layers of the quilt sandwich even with the quilt top edge. Using clear thread and a long, narrow zigzag stitch, machine baste the edges of the quilt sandwich all the way around the very outside edge.

2. Measure the height plus the width of the quilt, multiply by 2, and add 10″. This is the length of trim you will need.

3. Fold trim in half all along its vertical length, pressing as you go.

4. Starting at the lower right corner of the quilt, slip the folded trim over the edge of the quilt, pushing it into place so the fold is flush against the quilt edge. Pin into place, all around the perimeter of the quilt.

 Tip

● For slightly rounded corners: Trim the corners of the quilt so they are rounded. The trim can more easily and smoothly go around a curve than a square corner.

● For square corners: Pin the trim all the way around the quilt, then go back and fold in the miters at the corners, pin, and whipstitch closed.

5. After pinning, trim off the excess trim, leaving 1″ extra. Fold under the end and slip it over the trim end you started with. Pin in place.

6. To attach by machine, use clear thread in the top and bobbin (or thread that matches the trim), appliquéing through all layers with a machine zigzag stitch. Go slowly, checking to make sure you are catching the front and the back edges of the trim. Adjust the pinning if necessary. You can layer a second trim after the first is sewn on, too.

To attach by hand, use a whipstitch along the trim or lace edge, first on the front and then on the back.

 Note

You can also turn under the edges of the trim and sew on as with a traditional binding, as in *I Dream in Pink* (page 107).

Trim binding with ribbon

Trim binding with lace

FRENCH FACING (OR KNIFE-EDGE)

Visually, sometimes you don't want a binding. French facing will give a quilt a crisp finished edge with no narrow outline. *For Love of Asia* (page 50) and *My Washougal Dream* (page 112) use this method. Use a very thin fabric for the facing to reduce bulk. Lightweight silk habotai is a good choice. Allie thanks Tracey Brookshier for sharing this technique with her.

French facing

Preparing the Quilt and Facing

1. Mark the outer edges where you will trim the quilt.

2. Machine baste around the quilt, ⅛" inside that marked edge. The stitching will keep the quilt's layers from shifting while you are pinning and then sewing the facing strips and corners.

3. Trim on the marked line.

4. Measure the width and height of the quilt, and cut 2 strips of each length *minus 1"*, twice the finished width you want. (You may make the width any size, but it should be at least 1" wide after folding.)

5. Fold each strip in half lengthwise with right sides together, and press.

6. Cut 4 squares twice the width of the unfolded facing strips. (For example, a 4" unfolded strip requires an 8" square.)

7. Fold each square diagonally to make a triangle, and press.

Applying the Facing

1. On the front side of the quilt, pin a corner triangle into place, aligning the right angles of the corner with the edges of the quilt's corner. Machine baste along the very outer raw edges of the corner, in the seam allowance, to keep all layers from shifting. Repeat with the remaining 3 corner triangles.

2. Pin the first folded strip with the raw edges lined up with the edge of the quilt and the fold toward the center. The strip should end about ½" from the corner, overlapping the basted corner triangle.

3. Pin the remaining 3 strips into place in the same way. The ends of the strips will overlap each other.

4. Using a ¼" seam allowance, sew around the perimeter of the quilt. Trim the corner seam allowances at 45° angles.

Front of overlapped facing strips sewn into place over folded corner triangle. The corner of the quilt is trimmed ¼" at 45°. You can see the fabric triangle just peeking through at the corner.

5. Turn the facings to the back of the quilt. Press into place from the back and pin, making sure the ends of the facing strips are tucked under the corner triangle.

6. Whipstitch into place.

Finished corner, back view

Quilt Labels

As with all the projects in this book, we hope you will add a label to the back of your quilt, giving your name, the location where you made it, and the year, for future generations.

Label for *My Washougal Dream*

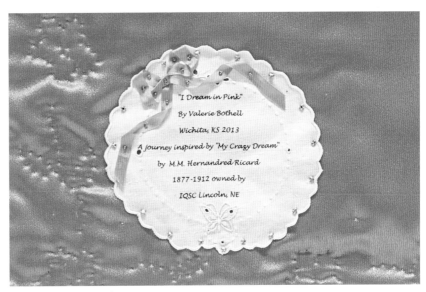

Label for *I Dream in Pink*

Stitching and Embellishing

Val Hand Embroidery

I love everything about crazy quilting, but hands down, my favorite part is the hand embroidery! For me, it is the great reward after doing all the piecing, and it really begins to dress up a crazy-quilt block. What might have looked like a plain, ordinary block can turn into a real treasure when you spend a little time doing some handwork. When I taught my *Crazy-Quilt Stitch Sampler* to my students several years ago, I thought a piece of striped fabric would make it easier to learn the stitches. The stripes simulate seamlines on a crazy-quilt block, making this a good way to practice the stitches. All the stitches being demonstrated will be shown on striped fabric; you may do this as you practice, or you can go for it and start on a crazy-quilt seam!

> ### ✦ Tip
>
> When you embroider, the tension on the thread is very important. If you pull the thread too hard the fabric will pucker, and if you leave it too loose the stitches will not have a crisp look.

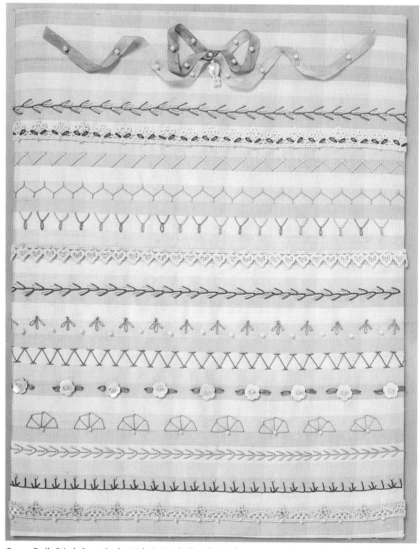

Crazy-Quilt Stitch Sampler by Valerie Bothell, 10″ × 13″

Crazy-Quilt Stitches

FLY OR Y-STITCH

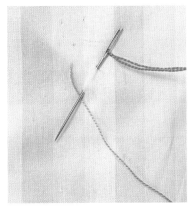

1. Bring the needle up on the left side of the stripe. Move the needle to the right and then slide it under the fabric at an angle. *Make sure the thread is under the needle as pictured.*

2. Pull the needle out from the fabric and gently pull the thread up, then down. Hold it in place with your left thumb.

3. Take the thread to the back of the fabric.

BASIC ALTERNATING FEATHER STITCH

1. Bring the needle up on the left side of the stripe. Move the needle to the right and then slide the needle under the fabric at an angle. *Make sure the thread is under the needle as pictured.*

 Tip

By varying the angle of the needle, you can make the feather stitch look completely different. Experiment with the angles and see how many different feather stitches you can make.

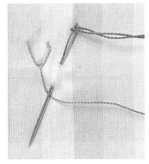

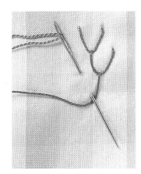

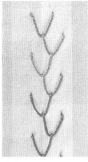

2. Pull the needle out from the fabric and gently pull the thread up, then down. Hold it in place with your left thumb.

3. Move the needle to the right and repeat Step 1.

4. Pull the needle out from the fabric and gently pull the thread up, then down, as you did before.

5. Move the needle to the left and repeat Step 1.

6. Continue as needed.

KNOTTED FEATHER STITCH

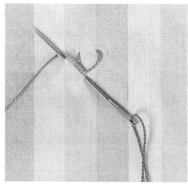  

1. Begin this stitch by following Steps 1 and 2 of the basic alternating feather stitch, and then take a stitch that starts at the base of the feather stitch and angles outward. Pull the needle toward you until the stitch is lying flat on the fabric.

2. Follow Steps 3 and 4 of the basic alternating feather stitch, and then repeat Step 1 of the knotted feather stitch.

3. Continue as needed.

BLANKET STITCH

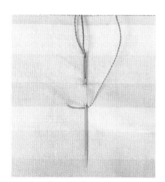 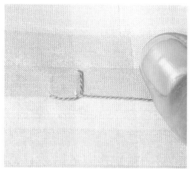 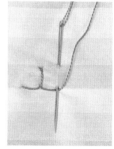 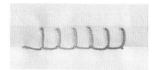

1. Bring the needle up on the lower edge of either a seam or the striped fabric. Move the needle to the right, placing it in a perpendicular position. *Make sure the thread is under the needle as pictured.*

2. Pull the needle out of the fabric and gently pull the thread to the right. Hold it in place with your left thumb.

3. Move the needle to the right and take a stitch in the same manner as you did before.

4. Continue as needed.

 Tip

You can change the look of the blanket stitch by varying the width and height of the stitch. Experiment and see the different looks you can come up with.

HERRINGBONE STITCH

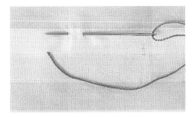

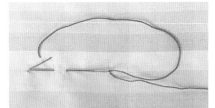

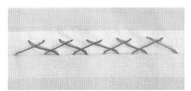

1. Bring the needle up on the lower edge of either a seam or a stripe. Move the needle to the right, and take a stitch on the upper edge of the stripe. *Make sure the thread is below the needle.*

2. Pull the thread out from the fabric. Move the needle to the right, and take a stitch on the lower edge of the stripe in the same manner as before. *Make sure the thread is above the needle.*

3. Continue as needed.

CHEVRON STITCH

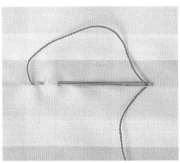

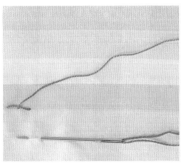

1. Bring the thread up on the edge of a stripe and move the needle to the right. Take a stitch halfway back to the left.

2. Pull the thread to the front of the fabric, making sure the thread is centered and below the stitch.

3. Move the needle to the right and down to the lower edge of the stripe. Take a stitch to the left.

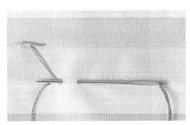

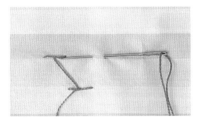

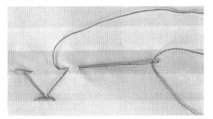

4. Pull the needle to the front of the fabric and move the needle to the right. Take a stitch back to the left, making sure the stitch is close to the thread that is in the center.

5. Pull the thread through to the front of the fabric, making sure the thread is centered and above the stripe. Move the needle to the right and up to the top edge of the stripe. Take a stitch to the right.

6. Pull the needle to the front of the fabric and move the needle to the right, staying on the top edge of the stripe. Take a stitch back to the left, making sure the stitch is close to the thread that is in the center.

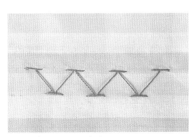

7. Continue as needed.

DETACHED CHAIN

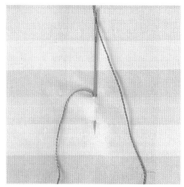

1. Bring the needle up on the edge of the stripe and take a stitch close to the thread, sliding the needle under the fabric.

2. Pull the thread to the front of the fabric.

3. Pull on the thread until you see the stitch form a loop. You can control the shape of this loop by the amount of tension you have on the thread.

4. Take the thread to the back of the fabric, stitching just on the other side of the thread that forms the loop.

CRETAN STITCH

To give you a good feel for this stitch, we will stitch it two stripe widths rather than the just one stripe width.

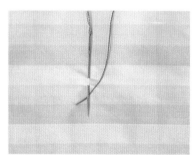

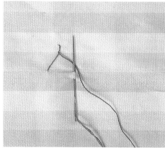

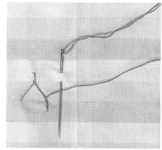

1. Come up on the middle line of the 2 stripes (if you are stitching on a crazy-quilt seam, come up on the seam). Move the needle to the right and take a ¼" stitch above the top stripe line. *Make sure the thread is under the needle.*

2. Move the needle to the right and take a ¼" stitch below the bottom stripe, making sure the thread is under the needle.

3. Move to the right and take a ¼" stitch above the top stripe, making sure the thread is under the needle.

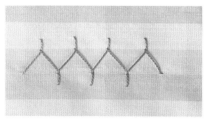

4. Continue as needed.

CRETAN/HERRINGBONE COMBINATION STITCH

One of the things that make crazy-quilt stitches so fun is the hundreds of ways that you can combine the stitches to make new ones.

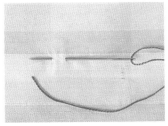 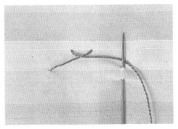 

1. Bring the needle up on the lower edge of either a seam or a stripe. Move the needle to the right, and take a stitch that is parallel to the upper edge of the stripe and moves from right to left. *Make sure the thread is below the needle.*

2. Move the needle to the right and take a stitch below the bottom edge of the stripe, making sure the thread is under the needle.

3. Move the needle to the right and repeat Step 1.

4. Continue as needed.

STEM STITCH

The embroidered house for *Oriental Garden* (page 90) was done almost entirely in stem stitch. For demonstration purposes the stitch will be done following one of the straight edges of a stripe.

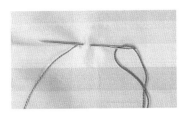 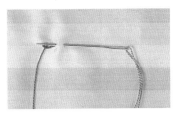 

1. Bring the needle up on the edge of the stripe and move the needle to the right. Take a stitch to the left, keeping the thread below the needle.

2. Pull the needle to the front of the fabric and move the needle to the right. Take a stitch to the left, keeping the thread below the needle, and come up close to the last stitch that you made.

3. Repeat Step 2 until you have completed the embroidery.

FRENCH KNOT

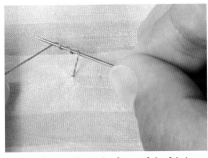 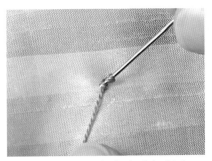 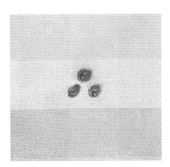

1. Bring the needle to the front of the fabric. Holding the needle in your right hand, take the thread in your left hand and bring it in front of the needle. Wrap the thread around the needle twice.

2. Take the needle to the back of the fabric close to where you came up, holding the thread in your left hand. Pull the French knot until it is snug against the fabric.

BASIC BULLION KNOT

I used this stitch to embroider the roses and rosebuds on *Oriental Garden* (page 90). It requires a milliners needle in a size 3 or 5, depending on the size of the thread.

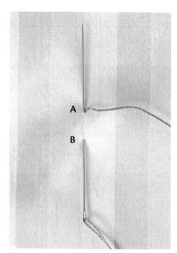

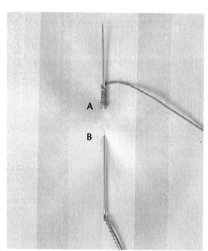

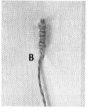
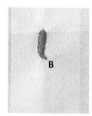

1. Pull the needle and thread to the front of the fabric at A. Take a stitch about ¼″ to B and push the tip of the needle to come out at A again, but do not pull the needle through the fabric. Hold the base of the needle and fabric in your left hand, pushing the tip of the needle up and away from the fabric. Pick up the thread coming out at A with your right hand.

2. Wrap the thread around the tip of the needle in a clockwise direction. The wraps around the needle need to be at least equal to the space between A and B.

3. When you have enough wraps on the needle, cover and hold the wraps with your left thumb and pull the needle through the wraps with your right hand, pulling the thread in an upward motion until the bullion wraps are nearly down to the fabric. Then pull the needle and thread toward B, laying the wraps flat against the fabric until there is no slack in the thread. Straighten any wraps that need straightening by rubbing your finger over them until they lie smooth. Push the needle and thread to the back of the fabric at B.

Silk Ribbon Embroidery

Both of us love to use silk ribbon embroidery in our work. It is a quick way to embellish a project and make it beautiful. In this section you will find the basic silk ribbon embroidery stitches we used in this book.

THREADING AND KNOTTING SILK RIBBON

Embroidering with silk ribbon is a little bit different than with thread. One big difference is the way you thread the needle and tie the knot on the end. For silk ribbon embroidery, it is best to use a size 22 or 24 chenille needle.

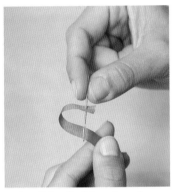

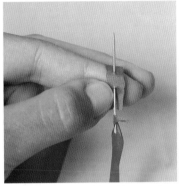

1. Thread the silk ribbon through the eye of the needle. Take the end of the ribbon and pierce it with the needle about ¼" from the raw edge. Pull on the long end of the ribbon to "lock" the ribbon into place on the eye of the needle.

2. To knot the end of the ribbon, grab the lower raw edge between your thumb and forefinger. Wrap the ribbon away from you around your forefinger. Take a stitch through the ribbon on your finger, starting about ¼" from the raw edge.

3. Pull the ribbon down over the eye of the needle and continue moving it down the length of the ribbon until a knot forms.

RIBBON STITCH

I've used this stitch to create flower petals and leaves.

 Tip

You may make the stitch any length to fit the project you are working on. To give the stitch a more natural look, ease some of the tension in the ribbon before piercing it with the needle.

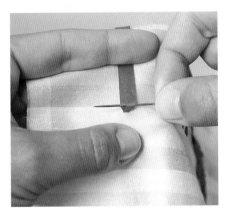

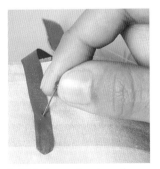

1. Bring the needle to the front of the fabric. Place the needle below the ribbon and, with slight pressure, move it toward the fabric. This will help to smooth out any wrinkles in the ribbon.

2. With the needle, pierce the middle of the ribbon about ½" from where it came out of the fabric. Pierce into the fabric as well.

3. Pull the needle to the back of the fabric until the ribbon comes to a point. Repeat to make a flower and leaves. Make a French knot in the center.

SIDE RIBBON STITCH

I used this stitch to make the silk ribbon cherry blossoms in *Oriental Garden* (page 90). The blossoms are a fun variation on the ribbon stitch flower.

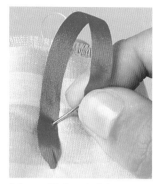  

1. Start with Step 1 of the ribbon stitch.

2. Pierce the right side of the ribbon with the needle.

3. Pull the needle to the back of the fabric gently until the ribbon comes to a point.

4. Repeat Step 1, bringing the ribbon up on the right side of the first stitch you did. Pierce the *left* side of the ribbon with the needle. Pull the needle to the back of the fabric gently until the ribbon comes to a point. Repeat to make a flower and leaves. Make a French knot in the center.

STRAIGHT-STITCH SILK RIBBON FLOWER

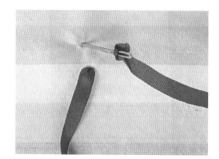 

Bring the needle to the front of the fabric and take a stitch ¼" away, leaving the ribbon loose. Repeat to make a flower and leaves. Make a French knot in the center.

SILK RIBBON HERRINGBONE STITCH

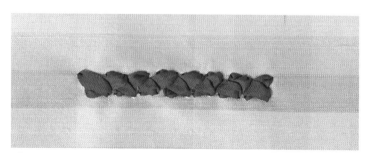

All crazy-quilt stitches can also be done using silk ribbon. *Color Block Fans* (page 98) has this herringbone stitch at the base of each fan. The stitches are very close together to get more coverage. When embroidering with silk ribbon, stitch with less tension than you would with thread, pulling gently on the ribbon and letting it lie softly.

Tips for Even Stitches

I love to make my stitches as even as possible, and over the years I have found a few things that help me get my stitching done more quickly. One of my favorite secret weapons is Tiger Tape, which comes in different widths and stitch sizes.

TIGER TAPE

Using Tiger Tape to make a chevron stitch. Not only can you make the diagonal line even by counting over four lines, but you can also make the bar on the top consistently the same size.

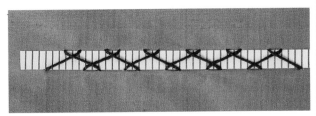

Using Tiger Tape to make a herringbone stitch

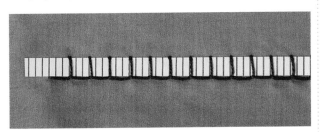

Using Tiger Tape to make even blanket stitches

One word of caution: Tiger Tape should not be used on velvets. It will pull the tufts of velvet out when you pull the tape off.

CRAZY-QUILT GRID TEMPLATES

Enclosed with her book, *Embroidered Crazy Quilt Seam Coverings*, Kelly Gallagher-Abbott has four templates called Crazy Quilt Grids that have also made my stitching much easier. In the following illustrations, I used a water-erasable pen for demonstration purposes, but I never use one on a regular basis because many of the fabrics I work with would not look good after getting wet. My usual marking pen is a purple air-erasable marker.

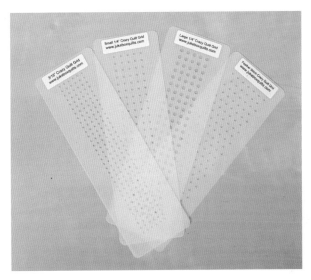

Using the template, mark the dots with the air-erasable pen. Stitch the chevron (page 35), herringbone (page 35), or blanket stitch (page 34) as usual, using the dots as a guide.

Chevron stitch

Herringbone stitch

Blanket stitch

Embroidery Transfer

There are many ways to transfer embroidery patterns. When I was working on *Oriental Garden* (page 90) I chose a fairly large embroidery pattern and didn't want to spend a lot of time tracing the whole image by hand onto tracing paper. By combining a copier, freezer paper, and traditional Golden Threads Quilting Paper (see Resources, page 118), I came up with a quick solution.

1. Cut both the freezer paper and the Golden Threads Quilting Paper to 8½″ × 11″.

2. Iron the Golden Threads Quilting Paper to the shiny side of the freezer paper, making sure there are no air bubbles.

3. Copy your embroidery pattern, running the freezer / Golden Threads paper combination through the copier as you would normally to make a copy. You want the pattern printed onto the quilting paper.

4. Let the ink dry and then carefully remove the Golden Threads paper from the freezer paper. Discard the freezer paper.

5. Baste the copy of the embroidery pattern in place, and you are ready to go!

 Tip

On washable fabric, another option is to use Wash-Away Stitch Stabilizer (C&T Publishing).

Hand Quilting

In *I Dream In Pink* (page 107) Val did some hand quilting around the border with silk twist thread. She used a size 3 milliners needle. The thread size and the thickness of the quilt will determine which needle you will want to use.

1. Trace the quilting pattern onto the fabric. Tie a knot in the end of the thread and take a stitch into the fabric about ½″ away from where you want to start. Instead of taking the needle to the back of the fabric, keep it in the batting that is in the middle of the quilt. Run the needle through the batting and bring it out to the front of the fabric on the quilting line. Gently tug on the thread until the knot goes through the top fabric and is buried in the batting in the middle.

2. Begin taking small stitches in and out of the fabric. When the needle gets full, pull it to the front of the fabric and start again, continuing until you have completed the quilting pattern.

3. If you come to the end of your thread before ending the quilting pattern, take a small stitch on the back of the quilt and take the thread through the loop that is formed. Pull the thread until a knot forms against the fabric, and bury the end of the thread in the layers of the quilt before snipping it off. Repeat Step 1 to start a new thread.

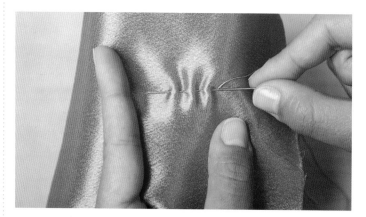

Machine Crazy-Quilt Embroidery ... Plus Some Handwork

Sometimes you just want to work on a crazy quilt faster than handwork allows. You can cut down on the time it takes to achieve complex-looking seam embroidery treatments that will "read" as handmade by using this simple approach: Sew a base of machine stitching and then add handwork stitches, beadwork, or even fabric paint. A bonus is that the spacing will be quite accurate, thanks to the even machine stitches.

There are both technical and aesthetic issues with this approach: In order to mimic hand-stitched seam treatments, you must be aware of the *scale* of the machine stitches. By scale I mean how complex the stitch is, how large, and how it proportionally fits into the space where it will be stitched. (For example, a large stitch is better on a longer seam, and a small stitch is better on a shorter one.) The scale will in turn determine the thread choice and weight, the needle size, and the upper thread and bobbin tensions. You must also choose and prepare the fabric properly for machine stitching.

With a basic understanding of these issues, we'll move on to the fun part: an extensive stitch sampler showing lots of machine/handwork combinations.

Finally, we'll try an easy exercise to get you familiar with this approach, with a super fast "pieced" crazy-quilt block for trying out the machine stitching. Once you've had a little practice, you will see what endless possibilities await you.

Crazy-Quilt Machine Embroidery Stitching

PREPARING THE FABRIC

Although many machine embroiderers hoop their fabrics before stitching, in this situation, I don't. These stitches are not heavy enough to warrant that, in my opinion, but if you feel more comfortable with a hoop, by all means use it.

Otherwise, *always* interface the fabric or sewn blocks you will be machine embroidering. Lightweight fusible knit interfacing prevents the fabric from puckering as you stitch. A double layer of interfacing stabilizes the fabric even more and is helpful on loosely woven fabrics. These layers do not impede the ease of hand stitching in the slightest.

There is not much point in machine embroidering crazy-quilt seam treatments on high-nap fabrics such as velvet, corduroy, burlap, or handwovens (all of which have their place in crazy quilting!). The nap just hides the threads. A very busy print will hide machine embroidery stitching, too, but any other fabric is suitable, as long as it is interfaced.

NEEDLES, TENSION, AND THREAD WEIGHT

Needles

A large-eyed needle helps reduce friction on the thread while sewing, thus preventing thread breakage. Jeans and topstitching machine needles are good. I personally prefer to use needles that are larger than my thread normally calls for. It just seems to make the sewing go more smoothly.

It's important that needles be sharp. Change them often during a long sewing project, as dull needles skip stitches much more often than sharp ones.

Thread Types and Weight

The weight, color, and fiber of the thread you use all contribute to the character of the stitch a machine will sew. Some threads are easier to work with than others, of course, with good-quality cotton threads the most commonly used for this kind of work. Silk and rayon threads add luster and sheen but are trickier to work with, so to introduce this subject we will stick with the more forgiving cottons. To see metallic threads in action, though, look at the sky section of *My Washougal Dream* (page 112).

Large-scale stitches show up beautifully in 12-weight thread. More intricate machine stitches work better with 28- or 40-weight thread.

Tension

Every machine is different, but normally when using heavier thread weights, you must loosen the upper tension so the thread can travel through the discs more freely.

If the top stitch is too loopy on the back, tighten the tension, and if it pulls up the bobbin thread to the surface or puckers the fabric, loosen it.

It is best to leave the bobbin tension as it is normally set during regular sewing.

Sewing Tips

- *Always* start with an interfaced stitching sample of the same weight as the quilt project. This is where you can play with the tension to get a smooth and secure embroidery stitch, as well as experiment with different stitch settings for length and width. Audition the threads, stitch settings, and tension on this sample before stitching on the project.

Stitch samples

- Make sure the bobbin is full before you start so you don't run out mid-seam. But if you do run out, clip stitches back to where a repeat starts, restart the machine, and reset the stitch so you can begin exactly where you left off. Keep sharp embroidery scissors and tweezers on hand just in case.

- Match the bobbin thread color to that of the top thread when possible. Otherwise, use a neutral color in a similar value. If specks of the bobbin thread show on the surface of the work, you can, oh so carefully, dot them with a fine-tip permanent marker in a color that matches the top thread.

- It is good to match the weight of the bobbin thread to that of the top thread, except in the case of 12-weight embroidery thread; 12-weight in the bobbin is too bunchy for all but the simplest stitches, and totally unnecessary.

- Always leave a 6″ to 8″ thread tail at the beginning and end of each row of stitching. This will enable you to easily bring the tails to the back of the work to knot off. A self-threading needle makes this job go quickly.

- The extra thread in the tail can also be used to go back and fill in skipped machine stitching by hand.

- Sew *slowly* when using heavier-weight threads (or delicate ones like metallic). If you go too fast, it can affect the tension, cause thread breakage, or cause distortion of the stitch pattern, especially when stitching along a curve.

- Embroidering over multiple layers (where several patches come together) can also cause distortion in the machine stitching. If the embroidery clumps up into too much of a blob to take out, you can always cover it with a little appliqué …

Blue appliquéd cherries cover an embroidery boo-boo on *Morning Chores* (page 82).

SOME GREAT CRAZY-QUILT MACHINE STITCHES

Almost all home sewing machines have built-in stitches you can use for embroidering seam treatments in crazy-quilt stitching. I am currently using my old Pfaff Quilt Expression 2048; it is nothing fancy. It does create stitches up to 9mm wide, which is helpful, but 6mm-wide stitches can be used too.

A rule of thumb is that the simpler and larger the stitch, the heavier the weight of thread you can use in the machine. Heavier thread in large stitching imitates the look of handwork, especially when the handwork you do add to it uses the same thread. The complex seam will "read" as entirely hand done.

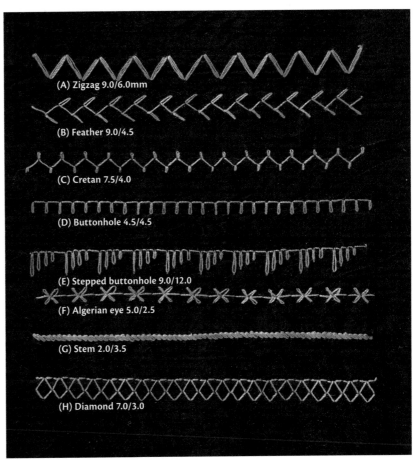

Figure 1. Large-scale machine stitches used alone or in combination with handwork, made with 12-weight embroidery thread in the top, 40-weight thread in bobbin, and a 100/16 jeans needle. Stitch length/width information is included, but your machine may vary.

Look over the machine, and you should find the following stitches, or some that are similar to the ones in the samples. All of these can look like crazy-quilt stitches, and no doubt you can find many more that will work too.

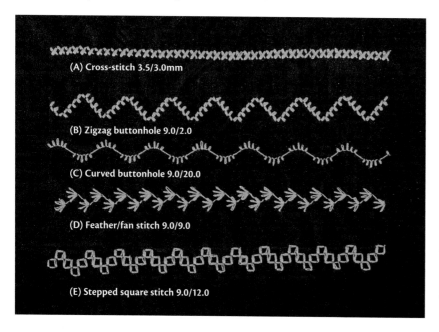

Figure 2. Smaller-scale machine stitches used alone or in combination with handwork, made with 28-weight thread in the top, 40-weight thread in the bobbin, and a 100/16 jeans needle. Stitch length/width information is included, but your machine may vary.

CRAZY-QUILT MACHINE STITCHING PLUS HANDWORK

Adding Hand Embroidery

You can get unlimited variation when you add some basic hand embroidery stitches to the machine stitches in Figure 1 (page 45) and Figure 2 (above). Refer to the hand embroidery stitches in Crazy-Quilt Stitches (page 33). Note that the same thread weight is used in both the machine and the hand embroidery.

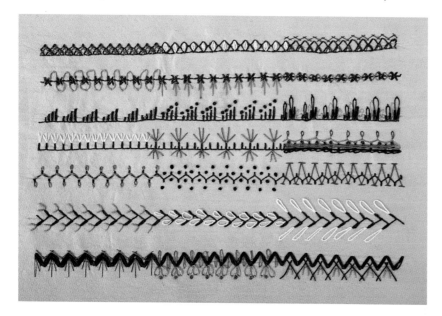

Hand stitches shown: French knot, lazy daisy, herringbone stitch, and chevron stitch. There is also some needle weaving, in which a loose thread is woven in and out of the bars of a blanket stitch, like a weft through a warp. Use the eye end of a threaded needle for the weaver's "shuttle."

Adding Beadwork

Adding seed beads is simple: Bring a beading needle threaded with Nymo or other strong beading thread to the front from the back of the work, string a bead onto the thread, and take the needle back down into the hole you came up through. This will cause the bead to stand up.

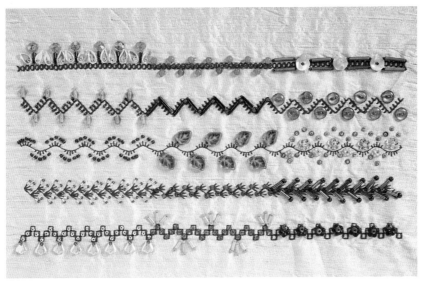

Beads added to the stitching in Figure 2 (page 46)

Larger beads need a bit more space between where the needle comes up to the work surface and where it goes to the back again, based on the size of the bead.

For bugle beads, add a small seed bead on the thread before and after the bugle, to prevent its sharp edge from eventually cutting the beading thread. Make sure you leave enough space between coming up and going back down with the needle for the seed/bugle bead combination to lie flat on the work.

The even spacing of the embroidery stitching by the machine makes hand beading so much fun … you don't have to worry about the spacing, so it goes quickly and is stress-free.

Adding Fabric Paint

You can add to the complex look of the machine stitching by painting inside the shapes that the machine makes for you. Any kind of fabric or acrylic paint will work; inks and dyes are too fluid, unless thickened—that is, unless you want the color to go outside the lines of the stitching.

Stars, hearts, fans, ovals, leaves, and flowers work well. When you add both hand embroidery and beading to these painted stitches, the results are detailed and unique.

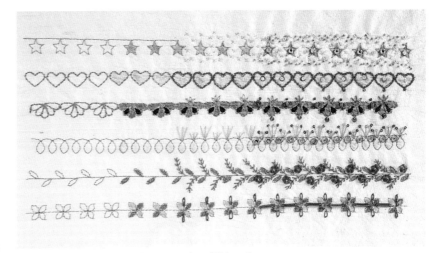

Each line of stitching shows the progressive addition of fabric painting, hand embroidery, and beadwork.

An Exercise in Crazy-Quilt Machine Embroidery

A no-sew crazy-quilt fabric collage provides the perfect canvas for practicing this embroidery approach. I'd like to thank the great quilt artist Susan Carlson for sharing her gluing ideas.

You Will Need

- 1 piece of muslin 10″ × 14″
- 1 piece of muslin 5″ × 8″
- 1 piece of sample cloth background 5″ × 8″
- 2 pieces of fusible knit interfacing 10″ × 14″
- 2 pieces of fusible knit interfacing 5″ × 8″
- Assortment of small scraps
- Assortment of 12-, 28-, and 40-weight machine embroidery threads
- Size 100/16 jeans needle
- Tacky glue, cardboard, and toothpicks
- Very sharp scissors
- Self-threading needle

Crazy-quilt collage in progress

Make a Stitch Sample Cloth

The stitch sample cloth will be used to try out the stitches for your collage before you actually stitch on your collage.

1. Fuse 2 layers of 5″ × 8″ interfacing to the back of the muslin 5″ × 8″ piece.

2. Layer the sample cloth background 5″ × 8″ piece on top of the muslin and baste the layers together. Set this aside until you are ready to try out some machine stitching on it.

Make the Collage

1. Fuse 2 layers of interfacing to the back of the muslin 10″ × 14″ piece.

2. Cut 3 or 4 fabric shapes and position them on the muslin. Sharp scissors will give a clean cut edge on these shapes. Fit them together with a scant ¼″ overlap along their edges.

3. Squirt a small amount of tacky glue onto the cardboard.

4. Gently pick up the first shape and dot the wrong side of its edges with tacky glue, using a toothpick. You don't need much glue, so the dots can be 1″ apart. Gently press the scrap into place. Dot the wrong-side edge of the second patch with glue, turn it over, and smooth it into place where it overlaps the first patch.

5. Continue cutting, fitting, gluing, and smoothing the collage elements in place until they cover the muslin.

6. Press the collage flat, carefully trimming any fabric "hairs" that might have come unraveled during the collage process.

Machine-embroidered crazy-quilt collage. What would you add to it?

Embroider the Collage

1. Choose a top thread, bobbin thread, and machine stitch, adjusting the tension and stitch settings (length or width) as necessary and desired. Practice on the stitch sample cloth until you're happy with the thread and stitch setting.

2. Embroider the first seam on the collage, leaving a 6" tail of thread at the beginning and end of the line of stitching. Remember to go slowly.

3. After the seam is machine embroidered, thread the tails individually into the self-threading needle, and then pull them to the back of the collage. Tie them off with the bobbin thread tail. Clip the knotted threads to ½". This prevents the machine stitching from coming out as well as preventing large thread blobs from forming on the back of the work. Doing this after each seam keeps the work neat.

4. Continue, filling in each seam with embroidery. It is good to change bobbin colors to match the top threads as you change those if you can; otherwise a medium-value neutral bobbin thread is fine.

This process just requires a little time and practice … but you will see with some experimentation that crazy quilting can go quickly yet still be true to form. And it is really, really fun.

EMBELLISHING TRIM AND PREMADE FLOWERS

By combining trims, edgings, or ribbon with some simple stitching, beadwork, or both, you can easily create a much more complex-looking trim. Use it as a seam treatment between patches or around the quilt as a visual "binding."

Fabric flowers, sold in craft stores or by millinery suppliers, are another easy way to give lovely three-dimensional interest to crazy-quilt work. They are used extensively in *My Washougal Dream* (page 112) and *For Love of Asia* (page 50).

This sampler gives just a hint of what is possible when combining trims, machine sewing, and handwork. All of these effects can be achieved quickly. Here's what I did.

A. On a ribbon base, I appliquéd premade silk ribbon trim, narrow metallic ribbon, and looped edging using clear thread in a zigzag stitch. I added a row of machine stem stitch in a 28-weight thread and hand herringbone stitch in 6-strand floss.

B. I used ½" fusible tape to layer 2 rows of rickrack and a ½" trim over a 1½"-wide woven trim. After fusing, I sewed everything down with clear thread in a zigzag stitch and added a row of beads down the center.

C. I fused lace over 13mm silk ribbon, again using fusible tape. I hand embroidered simple crosses in a straight stitch, using the patterns in the lace as guidance, with 6-strand cotton floss. I worked a Cretan/herringbone combination stitch (page 37) along the upper edge in size 12 silk perle.

D. With a machine basting stitch in clear thread down its center, I gathered 13mm silk ribbon, using 5 times the length of ribbon I wished the finished gathered length to be. I appliquéd it in place by machine using clear thread in a zigzag stitch, and then added evenly spaced premade flowers with a bead in the center of each. Refer to the frame in *My Washougal Dream* (page 112).

E. I layered combinations of premade fabric flowers and attached them with straight stitches, a large bead, and French knots.

For Love of Asia by Allison Aller, 29″ × 29″, 2012

This quilt uses all machine embroidery and hand beading
on its seams, and has some premade flowers beaded in their
centers, too.

For Love of Asia, detail

A Little Bit Crazy

Both of the beautiful and functional quilts offered here incorporate crazy quilting into a traditional quilt pattern. We hope this approach will entice quilters to go just a little bit crazy, adding just an element of embroidery along some of the seams, and a bit of crazy piecing ...

Val

Crazy Bow Ties

Finished size: 55″ × 62″ • **Finished Bow Tie block:** 5½″ × 5½″

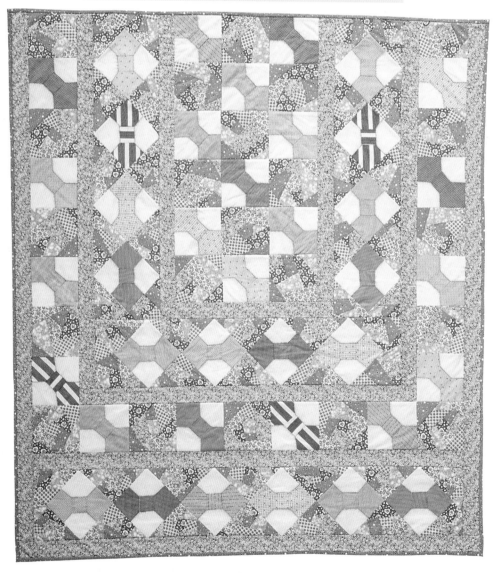

Crazy Bow Ties by Valerie Bothell, 2012

This quilt started with a plastic bag full of 92 vintage Bow Tie blocks I bought from an antique dealer. They were all hand pieced and none of them were the same size, but I still fell in love with them. Bow Tie blocks were popular in the 1930s, so it seemed only natural to use reproduction fabrics from the same era. This quilt is pieced directly to a microfleece blanket and is lap size, but it could be enlarged to fit any size bed. I machine embroidered all of the vintage squares to add a little more detail and further stabilize them.

What You Will Need

Yardage is based on 42"-wide fabric unless otherwise noted.

Blue print: 2½ yards for sashing and crazy blocks

Red print: 2 yards for binding and crazy blocks

Solid white: ¾ yard for Bow Tie blocks

4 different red and blue prints: ½ yard each for crazy blocks

9 different blue prints: ⅛ yard each for Bow Tie blocks

1 twin-size white sheet: (72″ × 102″) new or used, for foundation piecing

1 twin-size microfleece blanket: (72″ × 102″)

Please be sure to prewash all fabrics.

Cutting

All measurements include ¼" seam allowance.

Blue print:

(Cut from *length of fabric*.)

Cut 2 strips 2½″ × 60½″.

Cut 1 strip 2½″ × 55½″.

Cut 1 strip 2½″ × 51½″.

Cut 2 strips 2½″ × 43¼″.

Cut 1 strip 2½″ × 40½″.

Cut 2 strips 2½″ × 33½″.

Cut 1 strip 2½″ × 21″.

Use the remainder for crazy piecing.

Solid white:

Cut 7 strips 3¼″ × width of fabric; subcut into 78 squares 3¼″ × 3¼″.

Red print:

Cut strips for the binding method of your choice.

Use the remainder for crazy piecing.

Variety of blue prints:

Cut 78 squares 3¼″ × 3¼″. Cut these in matching pairs.

Cut 78 squares 2″ × 2″. Cut these in matching pairs.

Sheet:

Cut 4 squares 8″ × 8″; subcut diagonally into 8 triangles.

Cut 18 squares 6½″ × 6½″.

Cut 7 rectangles 6″ × 6½″.

Cut 54 squares 6″ × 6″.

Making the Bow Tie Blocks

Each Bow Tie block is made with 2 white 3¼″ squares and 4 matching blue print squares (2 squares 3¼″ × 3¼″ and 2 squares 2″ × 2″).

1. Mark a diagonal line on the wrong side of all the blue print 2″ squares using a washable marker of your choice.

2. Place a blue print 2″ square in a corner of a white 3¼″ square, right sides together. Sew a seam on the diagonally marked line. Trim to ¼″ past the seamline and press the seam toward the white fabric. Make 2 using matching blue squares.

3. Sew a matching blue print 3¼″ square to each of the units from Step 2 as shown and press the seam toward the blue fabric. Sew these 2 units together. Press.

> **Tip**
>
> Because the crazy blocks are foundation pieced, they have the weight of two layers. For this reason I lined the Bow Tie blocks with a 6″ square of the sheet fabric on the back of the block. The machine embroidery I did on the Bow Tie blocks is not only for decoration but also to attach the sheet fabric to the Bow Tie block.

4. Place a 6″ square of the sheet fabric on the back of the Bow Tie block and then embroider the block either by machine or by hand. Repeat Steps 2–4 to make 39 Bow Tie blocks.

Making the Crazy Blocks and Crazy Triangles

1. Using the 6″ squares of the sheet fabric as the foundation, piece 15 crazy blocks. Use the ½-yard cuts of red and blue prints, the remaining red print from the binding, and the remaining blue print from the sashing for the crazy piecing. Vary the piecing method using the Montano Centerpiece Method (page 14) and Montano Fan Method (page 15).

2. Using the 6″ × 6½″ rectangles of the sheet fabric as the foundation, piece 7 crazy blocks. Use the ½-yard cuts of red and blue prints, the remaining red print from the binding, and the remaining blue print from the sashing for the crazy piecing. Vary the piecing method using the Montano Centerpiece Method and Montano Fan Method.

> **Tip**
>
> I did half of my crazy blocks using the Montano Centerpiece Method and the other half using the Montano Fan Method because varying the piecing methods adds more interest to the blocks. Since the triangles were smaller and had been cut on the bias, I only used the Montano Centerpiece Method for them.

3. Using all the triangles cut from the sheet fabric as the foundation, piece 36 small crazy triangles and 8 large crazy triangles using the Montano Centerpiece Method (page 14).

Sewing the Quilt Together

Blocks are sewn into rows, and then the rows and sashing are sewn directly to the microfleece blanket as you sew it together, using the technique in Piecing Directly onto Backing (page 26). The quilt top is assembled starting at the top center and working down and out.

Sewing the Top Center Section

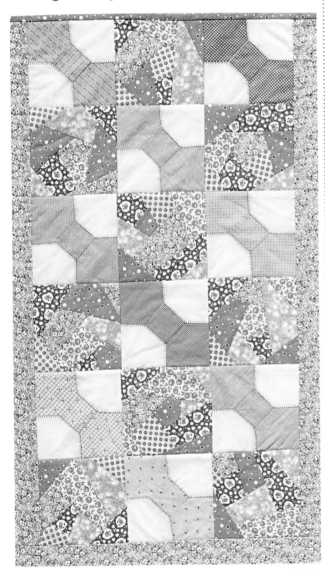

1. Sew a crazy 6″ × 6″ block between 2 Bow Tie blocks. Press the seams open. Make 3 rows like this.

 Tip

Make sure the Bow Tie blocks are all going the same direction as you sew the rows together.

2. Center a row at the top of the blanket, right side up and centered 2″ down from the hemmed edge of the blanket. Pin the row in place at the top and bottom long row edges, making sure the blanket underneath is smooth.

3. Sew a Bow Tie block between 2 crazy 6″ × 6″ blocks. Press the seams open. Make 3 rows like this.

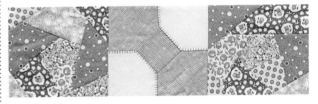

4. Line up a row from Step 3, wrong side down, on top of the first row of blocks (already pinned to the blanket). Make sure the block seams are aligned and the Bow Tie blocks are positioned in the same direction. Pin through all layers, including the blanket. Using a ¼″ seam, sew on the pinned lower edge through all layers.

5. Flip the second row of blocks to the right side and press smooth. Pin the lower edge of the blocks to the blanket, making sure it is smooth.

6. Repeat Steps 4–5 until you have attached 6 rows of blocks to the blanket, alternating the rows from Step 1 and Step 3 as you go. Keep all the Bow Tie blocks positioned in the same direction.

Sewing the Sashing in Place

1. Pin the 2½″ × 33½″ sashing strips on the sides of the center section through all layers. Lay a clear grid ruler on the raw edge of the sashing pieces to make sure they are straight. It is okay if the Bow Tie and crazy blocks are not perfectly straight on the outside edges; the sashing will hide that.

2. Sew through all layers, flip the sashing pieces to the right side, and press smooth. Then pin the loose edges to the blanket, making sure it is smooth underneath.

3. Pin the 2½″ × 21″ sashing strip on the lower edge of the center section. Refer to the tip on squaring up (page 27) for instructions on how to make sure that the sashing is squared up. Lay a clear grid ruler on the raw edge of the sashing to make sure everything is lying straight.

4. Sew through all layers. Flip the sashing piece to the right side, press smooth, and pin the loose edges to the blanket.

Sewing the Second Round of Blocks and Sashing

For the second round, the Bow Tie blocks are pieced on point with the crazy-quilt triangles that you have pieced. You'll sew the rows together and then sew the rows around the sashing you have just attached to the blanket.

1. Sew a small crazy triangle to each side of a Bow Tie block, placing the triangles in a diamond shape and noting the direction of the Bow Tie blocks as shown. Press the seams open. Make 12 diamond shapes.

2. For each row, sew 4 diamonds together, making sure the block seams are aligned. Press open. When you are done, the piece will look like a parallelogram. Make 3 rows.

3. Add a large crazy-pieced triangle at the top right and the bottom left corners of each row. Place the blocks so the longest edge of the triangle is where you will sew the seam. Press the seams open. Square up the ends of the rows. Make 3.

4. Trim the long edges of the rows as needed so you have a ¼″ seam allowance that extends past the white corners of the Bow Tie blocks; the ends of the rows will be trimmed later as needed.

5. Pin a row on the right side of the center section, lining up the straight edges, placing right sides together, and making sure the Bow Tie blocks are positioned correctly. Lay a clear grid ruler on the raw edge to make sure it is straight.

✦ Tip

When pinning the row in place, make sure the first white Bow Tie corner lines up with the first seam allowance in the center section. This assures that both sides of the second round will be aligned.

6. Sew the seam. Flip the row to the right side, press smooth, and pin into place, making sure the blanket underneath is also smooth.

7. Repeat Steps 5–6 to place the row on the left side of the center section. Trim the edges of the rows even with the section already sewn to the backing.

8. Match the center of the remaining row with the center section already sewn to the backing. Pin the row on the lower edge of the center section, lining up the straight edges, right sides together. The row will extend beyond the left and right sections you just sewed into place. *When pinning into place, check to make sure the 4 Bow Tie blocks are centered.* Use the same method you did with the sashing to make sure that the corners are squared up.

9. Sew the seam. Trim the ends of the row even with the rest of the section sewn to the backing. Flip the row to the right side, press smooth, and pin the loose edges to the backing, making sure the blanket underneath is smooth.

10. Refer to Sewing the Sashing in Place (page 56) and follow the instructions using the 2½″ × 43¼″ sashing strips for the sides and the 2½″ × 40½″ sashing strip for the lower edge.

Sewing the Third Round of Blocks and Sashing

The third round of blocks is sewn together with the Bow Tie blocks for the side rows going the same direction as they did in the center section. A row of Bow Tie blocks is sewn across the bottom to give the quilt further interest.

1. For each side of this row, refer to the quilt photo (page 52), arrange 2 crazy 6″ × 6½″ blocks, 2 crazy 6″ × 6″ blocks, and 4 Bow Tie blocks, alternating the crazy blocks and the Bow Tie blocks. Note the direction of the Bow Ties. (The position of the crazy 6″ × 6″ and crazy 6″ × 6½″ blocks doesn't matter as long as they alternate with the Bow Ties.) Sew the blocks into 2 rows. Press the seams open.

 Tip

When sewing these blocks together, make sure the Bow Tie blocks are going in the same direction as those in the center section. Lay them out around the second round to preview how they will look.

2. Position and pin the side rows to the sashing on the sides of the quilt center, as you have in the previous steps. Begin pinning the rows, starting at the bottom and working your way up. If there is excess at the top, you can trim that later. Lay a clear grid ruler on the raw edge to make sure it is lying straight. Sew. Flip the rows to the right side, press smooth, and pin the loose edges into place, making sure the blanket is smooth underneath.

3. For the bottom row, refer to the quilt photo (page 52) and arrange 4 Bow Tie blocks and 3 crazy 6″ × 6½″ blocks, alternating them and noting the direction of the Bow Ties. Sew the blocks together.

4. Add a crazy 6″ × 6″ block to each end of the row, and press the seams open.

5. Position this row on the bottom of the quilt. With right sides together, begin pinning the row, starting in the center and working your way to the outside. If there is excess at the ends, you can trim that later. Lay a clear grid ruler on the raw edge to make sure it is lying straight. Sew. Flip the row to the right side, press smooth, and pin the loose edges into place, making sure the blanket is smooth underneath.

6. Refer to the previous Sewing the Sashing in Place section (page 56) and follow the instructions using the 2½″ × 51½″ sashing strip, placing it on the lower edge of the section you just sewed in place.

Sewing the Last Row and Border

This is the last row. It will be sewn in place on the lower edge of the quilt and pieced in the same manner as the second round. Then sashing will go on 3 sides.

1. Referring back to the instructions in Sewing the Second Round of Blocks and Sashing, Step 1 (page 56), make 6 diamond shapes, using Bow Tie blocks and small crazy triangles, noting the direction of the Bow Tie blocks.

2. Sew the diamonds together and add a large crazy triangle to each end as before. Square up the ends of the row.

3. Pin this section in place, right sides together, on the lower edge of the sashing you sewed in place. Use a clear grid ruler to make sure that it is lying straight. Trim the edges of the row as needed.

4. Sew. Flip the row over and press smooth. Pin into place, making sure that the blanket is smooth underneath.

5. Refer to the previous Sewing the Sashing in Place section (page 56) and follow the instructions using the 2½″ × 60½″ border strips for the sides and the 2½″ × 55½″ border strip across the bottom.

Finishing

1. Square up by trimming away the excess blanket left around the edges. You may also trim away any excess from the crazy blocks that extends past the edge at the top of the quilt.

2. Bind the quilt, using the method of your choice, and enjoy!

Allie

Crazy for Plaid

Finished size: 72″ × 72″ • **Finished block:** 6″ × 6″

Crazy for Plaid by Allison Aller, 2012

In 2010, I saw an antique quilt in dealer John Saul's booth that completely knocked my socks off. I just *had* to make my own version of it. The pattern is called Gothic Windows.

This quilt is a great way to try out machine and hand embroidery. The quilt is tied with buttons, so there is no quilting. It really is just a little bit crazy.

There are strict design parameters at work here to keep construction simple and the quilt focused:
- Only one hand embroidery stitch and one machine stitch are used throughout the entire quilt.
- All the hand stitching is in shades of blue, and all the machine stitching is in shades of yellow.

- All the appliquéd shapes are in various black fabrics.
- All the background fabric squares are in the warm color range: almost no blues and very few greens.
- The buttons on the front are all yellow, and only two different sizes.

The repetitive hand stitching on the individual blocks means this project is portable, too. Once the blocks are embroidered, this quilt goes together fast because there are no borders or sashing. The binding has trim that covers its raw edges.

A Little Bit Crazy—Crazy for Plaid   **59**

What You Will Need

Yardage is based on 42"-wide fabric unless otherwise noted.

24 fabrics in wool, flannel, cotton, or silk: ¼ yard each for background squares (a total of 6 yards)

Various black fabrics: 3½ yards total (You can use scraps at least 3" × 9½".)

Backing: 4½ yards

Batting: 80" × 80" piece

1" black rickrack: 8¼ yards for front

½" black rickrack: 8¼ yards for back

121 yellow buttons: 1" diameter, 2-hole or shank, for front

144 yellow buttons: ½" diameter, 2-hole or shank, for front

265 buttons: any size and color, 2-hole, for back

Large assortment of blue embroidery threads and 4mm silk ribbons

Different yellow machine embroidery threads: 12 spools

Monofilament thread

Chalk marking pencil

Tracing and freezer papers

Yellow alcohol ink, small paintbrush *(optional)*

Cutting

All measurements include ¼" seam allowances.

Background fabrics:

Cut a total of 144 squares 6½" × 6½".

Black fabrics:

Cut a total of 144 strips 3" × 9½".

> **Note**
>
> If you have an AccuQuilt GO! fabric cutter, you can use the 6½" square die and the 3" strip cutter.

Making the Blocks

Preparing and Appliquéing the Lattice Pieces

1. Copy the *Crazy for Plaid* pattern (page 64) at 100%. Trace the lattice pattern shape several times onto freezer paper and cut the traced shapes out.

> **Tip**
>
> The reason I prefer using freezer paper as a template is that it doesn't slip when I am drawing around it, making it more accurate for me. However, you could make a cardstock template if you prefer.

2. Center the freezer-paper template ½" from an end of a black 3" × 9½" strip and iron in place on the right side of the fabric.

3. Mark around the template with the chalk marker.

4. Remove the template and cut out the lattice shape, leaving a ¼" seam allowance outside the marked line, but *cutting the right-angled corners on each end of the lattice flush with the marked line.* (After several uses, you will need a fresh freezer-paper template.) You will need 144 lattice pieces. You can cut and appliqué the lattice pieces individually, or you can cut out all 144 before starting to appliqué.

5. Iron under only the long, curved sides of the lattice pieces, using the chalk mark as a guide.

6. Pin the prepared lattice diagonally to a background square, matching its corners to the opposite corners of the background square.

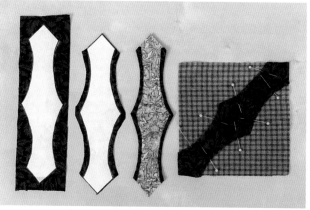

Prepare lattice pieces and pin to square.

7. Using clear monofilament thread in a zigzag stitch set to 2.5mm wide and 1.5mm long, appliqué each folded side of the lattice to the square, removing pins as you go. Refer to Pain-Free Sewing with Invisible Thread (page 10).

8. Sew in a straight stitch around the perimeter of the block ⅛″ from the edge to prevent the fabric from fraying.

Embroidering the Blocks

Use a herringbone stitch (page 35) to embroider over the appliquéd seams on each side of the lattice, using several different blue threads or ribbons throughout the quilt.

Embroider herringbone stitch around lattice piece.

That's it. By the time you finish 144 blocks, you will have mastered that herringbone stitch!

Assembling the Quilt Top

Play with the blocks' arrangement on a design wall or the floor, moving them around until you get a composition you like.

You will add the yellow machine embroidery as you go.

1. Trim the blocks to remove any stray threads and give them a clean edge.

2. Sew 2 blocks into a pair and then join 2 pairs, using a ¼″ seam, to make a square unit of 4 blocks. The lattice strips should form a "window" in the center of this unit.

3. Turn over the unit and press the seams open. This extra layer provided by the seam allowances will act as a stabilizer, improving the quality of your machine embroidery later. The pressed-open seam also ensures that the bulk is even on either side.

4. If you have ended up with spare or reject blocks, sew them together, iron open the seams, and test out the machine stitching to see how it looks between the blocks. Otherwise, make a quick sample cloth to choose the stitch type, length, and width, and to adjust the tension as needed. Refer to Crazy-Quilt Machine Embroidery Stitching (page 43). Remember that all the machine embroidery is done with yellow threads.

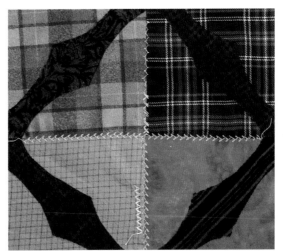

Sample stitching on rejected 4-block unit

5. Starting at the outer end of the first seam, stitch toward the center of the unit in your chosen stitch and thread. Be sure to leave a 6″ tail at the beginning and end of the seam. Repeat on each seam.

6. Bring the yellow thread tails to the back of the quilt top and knot off with their bobbin tails. Clip to ½″.

7. When you have embroidered the seams on all 4-block units, sew them together to make units of 8 blocks and repeat Steps 3–6.

8. Continue, sewing larger and larger units together and embroidering the seams, until the entire top is assembled and embroidered, with 12 blocks across and 12 blocks down.

Finishing

Making the Quilt Sandwich

1. To make the quilt backing, cut the length of backing fabric in half from selvage to selvage, creating 2 pieces 2¼ yards long. Trim off the selvages before sewing the pieces together lengthwise, and press the seam open. Trim to 80″ × 80″. Reserve the extra backing fabric; you will use it for the binding later.

2. On a large flat surface (I like to use a folding 30″ × 72″ table), lay out the quilt back, right side down, then the batting, and then the quilt top, right side up.

3. Pin baste the quilt sandwich together, with a pin in every other block.

Tying the Quilt with Buttons

You will add the large buttons on the intersections of the blocks. Mark the center of each lattice piece with the chalk. You will position and add the small buttons on these marks. Refer to Buttoned (page 24). The buttons are sewn on in pairs, a button each on the front and back of the quilt. I like to use that large folding table for this work, rolling the quilt up tightly as I work my way toward the center of the quilt to give myself access to the middle area, sewing on the pairs of buttons.

 Tip

If you are using mother-of-pearl buttons and want to change their color, alcohol inks are magical. Simply spread a small amount of the color you like onto the surface of the button with a paintbrush. The button absorbs the color instantly and permanently, without losing its shine. If the color looks too intense to you, blot the ink quickly with a paper towel before it dries. When finished, clean the brush with running water.

Alcohol ink being applied to mother-of-pearl buttons

1. Pair up a yellow 1″ button for the front with a 2-hole button of any size or color for the back. Working from the front of the quilt, knot the thread and bring the needle into the center of the first intersection on the quilt top and through to the back of the quilt.

2. Flip the quilt over so the back is facing up. Slide the needle through a hole of the back button and return the needle through the second hole of the back button, making sure you come up right through the center of the intersection between the blocks.

3. Slide the needle through a hole of the yellow 1″ button (in my quilt's example, through the shank on the back of the button). If using a 2-hole button, return the needle through the other hole to the back of the quilt through the seam intersection, with the needle emerging through a hole in the back button.

4. Continue sewing between the holes in the pair of buttons, back to front, front to back, until both buttons are securely sewn on (about 8 passes). Make a small knot under the edge of the button in the back, and cut off the thread close to the knot.

5. Repeat until all 121 large button pairs are in place at the block intersections. Then sew on the 144 front yellow ½" buttons paired with backing buttons of any size and any color, in the marked centers of the lattice strips. This is a very good time to have a long TV miniseries to keep you company as you work, or a good audiobook.

Binding

This binding has its raw edges covered on each side by hand-appliquéd rickrack. Refer to the corner detail.

Front corner detail

1. Trim the quilt sandwich so the batting and backing extend ½" beyond the edge of the quilt top.

2. From the length of the excess backing, cut 4 strips 2½" × 80". Fold each strip in half lengthwise with wrong sides together, and press.

3. Insert a binding strip over the edge of the first side of the quilt so the crease in the strip is flush with the edge. Pin into place.

4. With a matching thread, use a wide zigzag to stitch through all layers of the binding and quilt sandwich to attach the binding strip. Make sure that the raw edges on both sides of the quilt are within the zigzag. Trim the ends of the strip even with the edges of the quilt.

5. Repeat on the opposite side of the quilt.

6. Use another binding strip and miter its end by folding each corner toward the inside center at a 45° angle. Pin the mitered edge to overlap the binding strip already sewn to the quilt. Continue pinning the new binding strip to the quilt as before. Cut off the excess length of the strip just beyond the corner, and repeat the mitered folding and pinning to enclose the corner. Zigzag the pinned edges through all the layers.

7. Repeat Step 6 for the last side of the binding. Then whipstitch the mitered corners closed.

8. On the front of the quilt, starting just past a corner, pin the large rickrack into place, covering the raw edge of the binding. Round the corners with the rickrack, and continue around the quilt. Clip off the excess rickrack 1" beyond where you started and fold under the end, overlapping the raw edge of the rickrack.

9. Hand appliqué both edges of the rickrack with a small stitch in each peak and valley.

10. Repeat Steps 8–9 for the smaller rickrack along the raw edge of the binding on the back of the quilt.

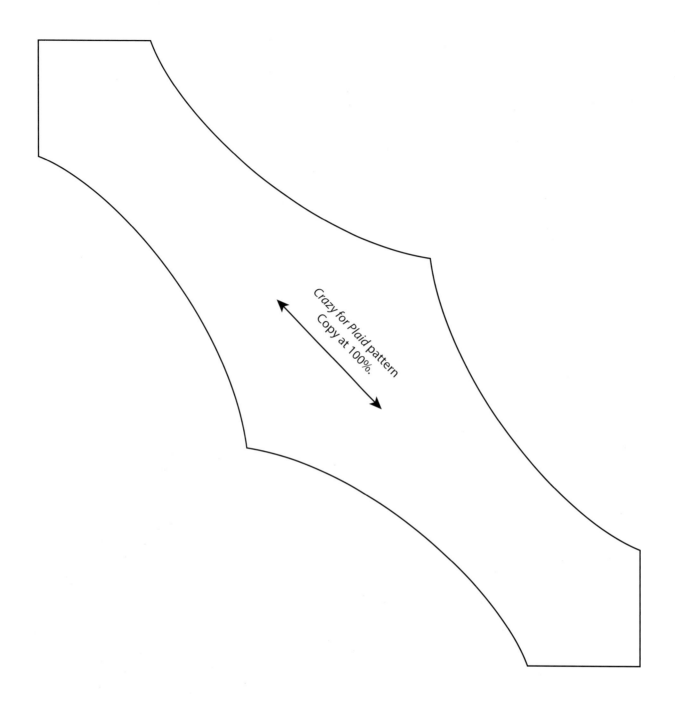

Crazy for Plaid pattern
Copy at 100%.

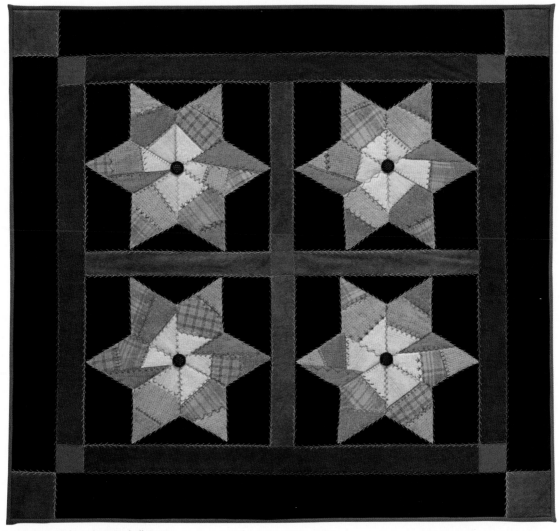

Amish Wool Crazy

Many Amish quilts are scrappy, but what surprised us is that a few Amish quilters did make wool crazy quilts. Both of our quilts use many of the traditional colors found in Amish quilts, but we've also used contemporary hand-dyed wools and plaids. Val's quilt is a wallhanging with hand embroidery and Allie's is twin-bed size, incorporating lots of machine quilting with hand embroidery.

Val

Amish Bouquet

Finished size: 45½″ × 41½″ • **Finished block:** 15½″ × 13½″

Amish Bouquet by Valerie Bothell, 2012

I looked at hundreds of Amish quilts to draw inspiration for *Amish Bouquet*, and my eye was always drawn to the star blocks. Many of these star blocks were crazy pieced, but some were not. Because the wool I used for this project is fairly heavy, it couldn't be pieced using conventional ¼˝ seam allowances. For this reason, the entire quilt was made by butting the raw edges of the wool together and zigzagging where they met. It was a new way of making a quilt for me, but I enjoyed every moment!

What You Will Need

Yardage is based on the noted width.

54˝-wide drapery lining: 1⅞ yards (I used ivory.)

60˝-wide black wool: 1½ yards for background and border

60˝-wide bright mauve wool: ½ yard for cornerstones and binding

60˝-wide purple wool: ⅜ yard for sashing

60˝-wide teal wool: ¼ yard for sashing and cornerstones

60˝-wide gold wool: ⅛ yard for flowers

60˝-wide mauve/pink wool: ⅛ yard for flowers

60˝-wide blue wool: ⅛ yard for flowers

60˝-wide purple wool: ⅛ yard for flowers

60˝-wide green wool: ⅛ yard for flowers

60˝-wide wool: 1½ yards for backing and hanging sleeve

Cotton batting: 47˝ × 47˝ piece

4 black buttons

Monofilament thread

Perle cotton: 8 colors, to coordinate with the wools

Cutting

Copy the Amish Bouquet *pattern (page 70) at 100%. Trace the pattern onto cardstock and cut on the lines to make a template for cutting diamonds from the drapery lining. No need to worry about any seam allowances in the project.*

Drapery lining:

Cut 1 square 49˝ × 49˝.

Cut 24 diamonds, using the *Amish Bouquet* template.

Black wool:

Cut 4 squares 16˝ × 16˝.

Cut 2 strips 4˝ × 37½˝.

Cut 2 strips 4˝ × 33½˝.

Bright mauve wool:

Cut 4 squares 2¼˝ × 2¼˝.

Cut 1 square 2˝ × 2˝.

Cut strips for the binding method of your choice.

Purple wool:

Cut 2 strips 2¼˝ × 29˝.

Cut 2 strips 2¼˝ × 33˝.

Teal wool:

Cut 4 squares 4˝ × 4˝.

Cut 2 strips 2˝ × 15½˝.

Cut 2 strips 2˝ × 13½˝.

Backing fabric:

Cut 1 piece 50˝ × 46˝.

Making the Crazy-Quilt Diamond Flowers

I positioned some of the wool fabrics in key places to make the six diamond shapes look like flower petals in the block. At the end of each diamond petal, I made sure there was a yellow piece of wool for the center, and I placed green wool on the opposite edges of two of the diamonds to make the leaves for each flower. The two green leaf diamonds have four pieces: the green, the yellow, plus two additional colored pieces. The other diamond petals are pieced with three pieces: the yellow, plus two additional colored pieces. Refer to the quilt photo (page 65) to see the diamond petals.

Tip

This entire crazy quilt is made using invisible thread with a zigzag stitch. Refer to Pain-Free Sewing with Invisible Thread (page 10). It will be worth the time to get completely comfortable with this technique before starting.

When piecing the wool together, it is important that the edges be perfectly straight. You may even want to put a new blade in your rotary cutter before you start in order to get a cleaner finish where the fabrics join.

1. For the flower petals (no leaf green), design the shapes for piecing and cut them so they will fit together on the diamond foundation with clean, straight inside edges and the outside wool edges extending just beyond the diamond foundation. (The outside edges will be trimmed later.) Place a yellow piece on the bottom tip with 2 additional colors. Design 16 flower petals.

2. At the machine, lay the yellow piece side by side with a piece of a second color, on top of the diamond foundation and with the pieces right side up. Make sure the 2 pieces of wool come together directly below the needle and that the zigzag stitch is wide enough to catch both pieces of wool. Using monofilament thread, zigzag the pieces together. Repeat for the third piece to complete the petal. Make 16.

3. For the leaf petals, design the shapes for piecing and cut them so they will fit together on the diamond foundation with clean, straight inside edges and the outside wool edges extending just beyond the diamond foundation. (The outside edges will be trimmed later.) Design 8 diamonds with the yellow on the bottom tip, the green on the left tip, and 2 additional colors.

Tip

You can add more variety by adding more pieces to the diamond petals. Here I used five pieces.

4. As you sew these diamonds, lay the green piece on the diamond foundation. Position a piece so the straight edges are directly under the needle, as before, and zigzag the pieces together. Continue adding the additional pieces and zigzagging all the inside straight edges.

5. Turn the diamonds over and press. Working from the back and using a rotary cutter and ruler, trim the edges of all of the completed diamonds just even with the diamond foundation, so they all have a nice sharp edge for the next step.

Sewing the Diamonds to Make Flowers

Notice how all the yellow pieces are in the center and the green leaves are on opposite sides of the flower.

1. Lay out the diamonds to make the flowers, with the leaves in the proper position, on the 4 black 16″ × 16″ squares. Move the different diamonds around until you have a good balance of color in the flowers. You will trim the black background later.

2. Lay 2 diamonds, side by side, on top of the black square, making sure the yellow ends are in the center of the black square. Pin in place and zigzag the 2 pieces together where they adjoin, using invisible thread.

3. Continue sewing the diamonds into position on the seams that adjoin, making sure the outer point of each diamond lines up with the diamond across from it.

4. Check again that the outer points of the diamonds line up across from each other, and pin the outer edges in place. Sew the entire outer edge of the flower shape down, using the invisible thread and a zigzag stitch. Make 4 blocks.

5. Embroider all the seams and the outer edges of all 4 flowers. Refer to Stitching and Embellishing (page 32).

6. Refer to the quilt photo to check the position of the diamond flowers. Trim the blocks to 15½″ wide and 13½″ high. Do the trimming very carefully because this is your only chance. Make sure the trimmed edges are as sharp as possible.

Assembling the Quilt Top

1. Draw the quilt grid (page 69) on the 49″ square of drapery lining, using a ruler and fine-tip marker. None of the markings will show on the finished quilt. Measure precisely and ensure that all the 90° angles are accurate. You will use this drapery square as the foundation for the quilt.

2. Refer to the red numbers on the grid. Beginning with pieces 1 and 2, position and pin the pieces onto the grid. Bring the edges together and sew the pieces to the foundation as you did when you pieced the diamond petals. Use monofilament thread and a zigzag stitch wide enough to catch the edges of both fabrics as you sew the pieces together.

3. Continue to join the pieces together in numerical order.

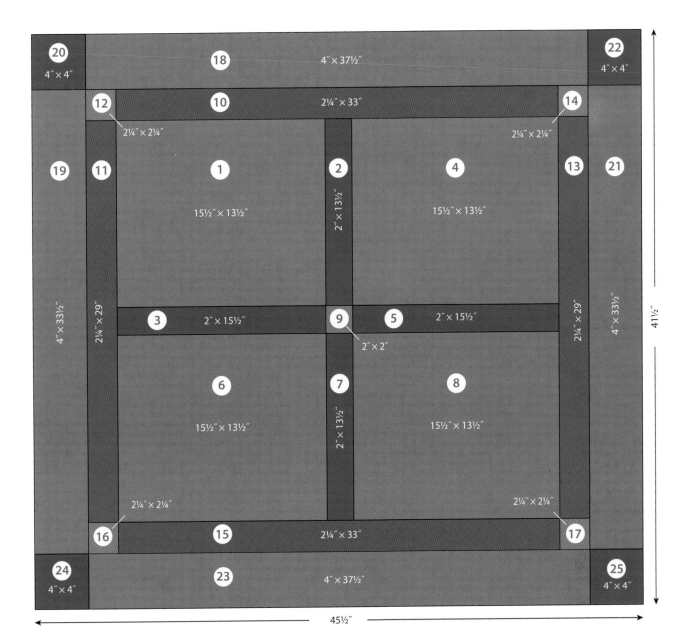

Finishing the Quilt

1. Before layering the quilt, hand embroider all the sashing and block seams using the basic alternating feather stitch (page 33) in a contrasting thread.

2. Layer the quilt top, batting, and backing. Use the technique in Interior Tying Method (page 24) to tie the quilt.

3. Trim any excess fabric around the outer edges and bind, using the method of your choice.

4. Sew the black buttons to the flower centers and add a hanging sleeve to the back of the quilt.

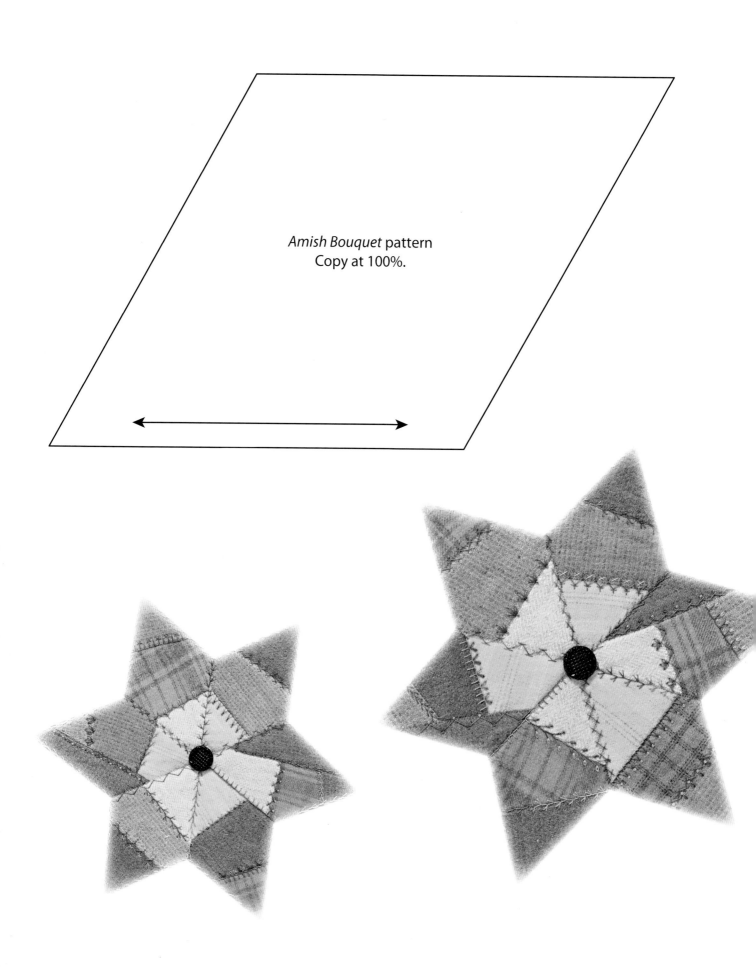

Amish Bouquet pattern
Copy at 100%.

Ode to the Amish

Finished size: 65″ × 83″ • **Finished block:** 6″ × 6″

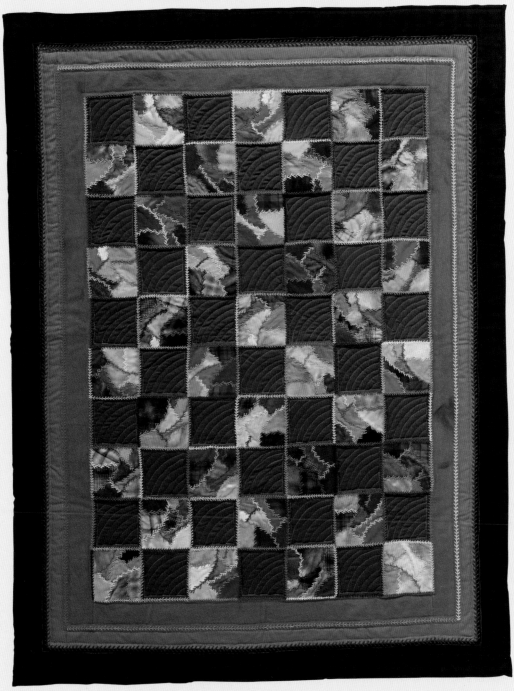

Ode to the Amish by Allison Aller, 2013

I love this design because of the great graphic impact and also because it gives ample scope for crazy patchwork, hand embroidery, *and* machine quilting. It has long been my goal to combine these techniques in a crazy quilt in such a manner that they bring out the best in each other ... and it was the Amish who showed me the way.

What You Will Need

Yardage is based on 42"-wide fabric unless otherwise noted.

Blue wool: 1⅓ yards for plain blocks

Muslin: 1⅞ yards for crazy block foundations

Various colors of hand-dyed wool: 2 yards total for blocks

Purple wool: 2 yards for inner borders

Dark blue wool: 6 yards for outer borders, backing, and fold-over binding

Wool batting: 71" × 89" piece

Heavy silk and/or wool crewel embroidery thread: 30 colors

Large-eyed chenille embroidery needle

Self-threading needle

Chalk fabric marker

1 bottle of Rit purple dye

1 bottle of Jet-Dry dishwasher water conditioner

White vinegar

Cutting

All measurements include ¼" seam allowances.

Muslin:

Cut 35 squares 7¾" × 7¾".

Blue wool:

Cut 35 squares 6½" × 6½".

Making the Crazy Blocks

The pieced blocks all use the very same block design. It has been flipped and rotated in different directions to give plenty of visual variation while maintaining unity. Producing these blocks goes very quickly as you gain familiarity with the block's design.

Preparing the Foundations and Templates

1. Trace the *Ode to the Amish* pattern (page 75). Make a copy of the drawing, and then reverse the image and make a copy of that.

2. Trace both the original and reversed drawings onto freezer paper, numbering the shapes as shown. Mark the reversed block patches with an R after the number. Note in the photo below how an additional margin is drawn around the perimeter of the block. Be sure to include this extra margin when you trace the block pattern.

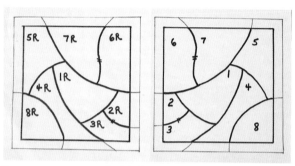

Freezer-paper patterns of original and reversed block designs

3. Lightly trace 17 of the original and 18 of the reversed block designs onto the muslin squares.

4. Cut apart the freezer-paper templates on the solid lines.

Appliquéing the Blocks

1. Iron the templates for a block onto your choice of colored wool fabrics and trace around them using the chalk marker.

2. Remove the templates and cut out the shapes, leaving at least a ¼" margin beyond the marked lines.

3. Refer to Freezer-Paper Template Appliqué (page 7). Place patch 1 in place on the marked muslin. Iron under the overlapping edges of the subsequent patches and appliqué them to the foundation in numerical sequence. Use clear thread in a zigzag stitch. Refer to Pain-Free Sewing with Invisible Thread (page 10).

4. Machine baste ⅛" from the edge of the block around the perimeter to stabilize the block for embroidery. Make 35.

Embroidering the Crazy Blocks

The embroidery is quite simple, in keeping with the Amish sensibility. Only 2 stitches are used throughout the quilt: the basic alternating feather stitch (page 33) within the blocks and the fly stitch (page 33) between the blocks and the borders. You will know both stitches well when you are done!

1. Embroider the blocks using the basic alternating feather stitch (page 33). I used a heavy single-ply silk thread, a large needle, and big stitches. When using the feather stitch on the crazy blocks, alternate with 2 stitches in one direction and then 2 stitches the other direction as you work your way through the block.

Note

At this stage, the quilt is a great portable project; it is easier to embroider the small blocks before you assemble the quilt top.

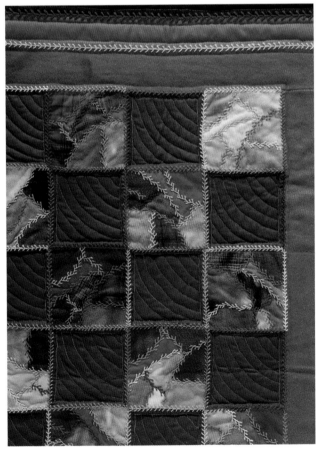

Detail of block embroidery

2. Iron the blocks from the back, and then trim them to 6½″ × 6½″.

Assembling the Quilt Top

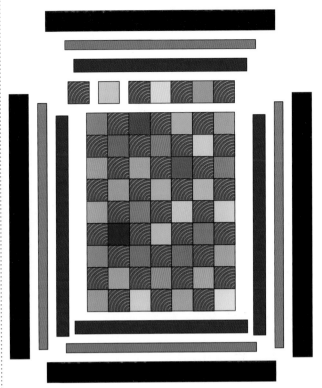

Quilt layout and quilting

Center Section

Use a ¼″ seam allowance.

1. Referring to the quilt photo (page 71) and the diagram above, sew 5 rows alternating 4 solid blue blocks with 3 pieced blocks. Then sew 5 rows alternating 4 pieced blocks with 3 solid blue blocks.

2. Arrange the quilt center, alternating the rows from Step 1. Sew the rows together.

3. From the back, press all the seams open.

4. Using the fly stitch (page 33) in wool yarn, embroider each of the seams between blocks.

Borders

OVERDYEING THE INNER BORDER WOOL

As long as you don't "shock" the wool fibers by giving them too sudden a temperature change, overdyeing wool in a solid color is not hard to do. Presoaking the wool in a solution of water and Jet-Dry helps the wool absorb the dye and gives a more saturated color.

1. Cut an 18″-wide section the entire length of the purple wool to overdye.

2. Fill the kitchen sink, a clean large bucket, or a 2-gallon pot with warm water and add the Jet-Dry liquid. Mix well.

3. Submerge the purple wool strip in the solution and let sit for 15 minutes, agitating occasionally.

4. Remove the wool from the solution, discarding the liquid. (Do not rinse.) Refill the container with warm water and follow the complete instructions on the Rit dye bottle. (They will recommend you add vinegar to the dye bath.)

5. Allow the dyed wool to air dry—do not put in the dryer. The result should be a shade of purple darker than what you started with.

6. When the wool is dry, iron it using the wool setting of an iron with no steam.

CUTTING, ADDING, AND EMBROIDERING THE BORDERS

1. From the length of the overdyed purple wool, cut 2 strips 4″ × 51″ and 2 strips 4″ × 62″. (I like to have a little extra when I cut border lengths, and then trim them to fit after sewing them on.)

2. Sew the long strips to each side of the center section, trimming the ends flush.

3. Sew the short strips to the top and bottom of the center section, again trimming the ends flush.

4. From the length of the purple wool, cut 2 strips 3″ × 56″ and 2 strips 3″ × 69″.

5. Sew on the middle border as in Steps 2–3.

6. From the length of the dark blue wool, cut 2 strips 6″ × 67″ and 2 strips 6″ × 74″.

7. Repeat Steps 2–3 to add the outer border.

8. Press the seams from the back.

9. Embroider between the border seams with a fly stitch (page 33).

Finishing

Quilting

1. From the remaining dark blue wool, piece the backing to be 71″ × 89″.

2. Place the backing right side down, layer the batting over it, and center the quilt top, right side up, over the batting/backing layer (I use the floor).

3. Pin baste in the center of each plain and embroidered square, and in the borders.

4. The pattern and method of quilting are up to you.

Based on a suggestion from the talented quilter Jamie Wallen, I quilted a line around the inside of each plain square and then filled each square in with a simple fan motif. This made the embroidered squares really pop out. I quilted on either side of the stitching in the borders as well, for the same effect.

I marked the wool with a chalk pencil. It showed up easily and brushed off quickly after the quilting was done.

I used a Sweet Sixteen machine by Handi Quilter, so all the quilting is free-motion, guided by hand. This design could easily be done on a home sewing machine as well, or you could hand quilt this project. Leave at least a 6″ thread tail at the beginning and end of each quilting motif or line, if quilting by machine. Use a self-threading needle to bring the thread tails to the back of the quilt. Tie the ends off and bury them inside the quilt sandwich, clipping off the excess when you bring the needle back out.

Detail of fan quilting in a plain block

Applying the Fold-Over Binding

1. Use the method in Fold-Over Binding (page 28). Trim the batting/backing layer to 1" beyond the edge of the quilt top. Fold the backing edge ½" so the raw edge meets the raw edge of the quilt top. Press. Then fold ½" again onto the quilt front. Use lots of pins to keep it in place. (I like to include the batting to give a nice, full, binding-like edge.)

2. Whipstitch it in place using a strong matching thread.

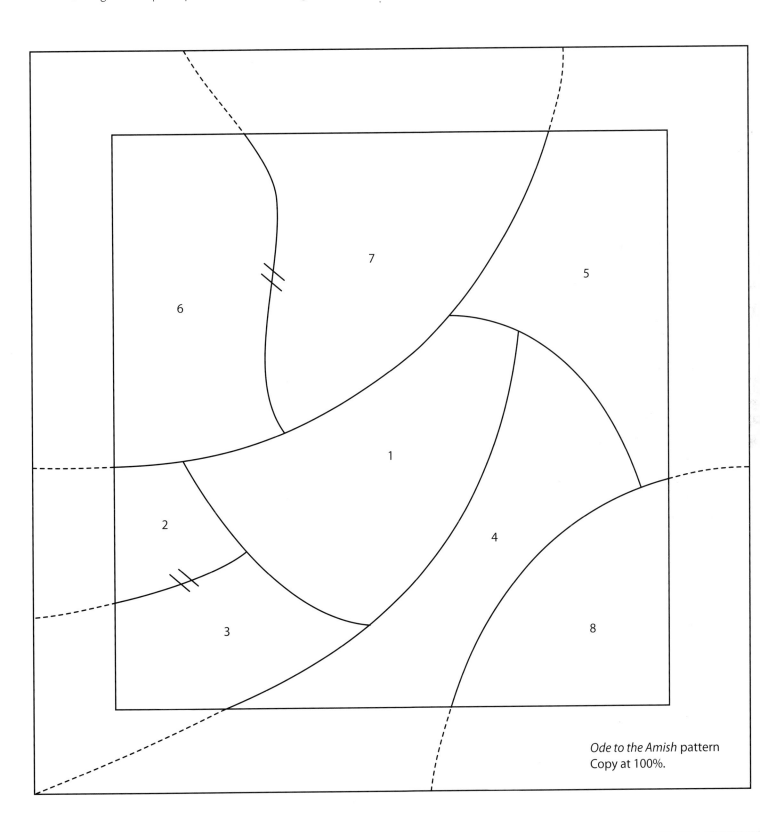

Ode to the Amish pattern
Copy at 100%.

Workingman's Crazy

Many older examples of crazy quilts were made with used fabrics such as shirting, overalls, and feed sacks. They have the random piecing we associate with the crazies but sometimes no embroidery at all. These country crazy quilts made by the farmwives of old really appealed to both of us. We inherited some charming vintage feed sacks that had once belonged to farmwife Gladys Evelyn Kurr, fondly known as Glady. She was a hardworking Kansas farmwife who loved her rose garden and had strong Christian values. She was a very warm and loving grandmother. We both incorporated her feed sack fabric into our quilts, and without it they wouldn't have been the beauties they became. Each is unique in its own way, with Allie using free-form appliqué and machine embroidery, and Val crazy piecing long strips.

Val

Fond Memories

Finished Size: 54" × 54"

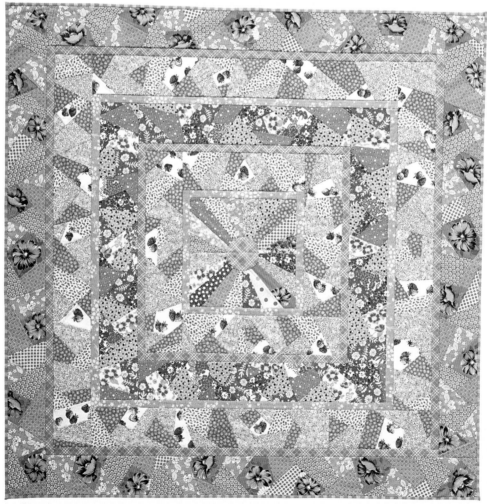

Fond Memories by Valerie Bothell, 2012

Val on her tricycle with Grandma Hansen, circa 1965

Photo: Valerie Bothell

This quilt began with Gladys's delightful feed sack fabrics and evolved from there. I decided to add 1930s reproduction feed sack fabric to the mix, and I also looked through my stash and found several lovely fabrics that belonged to my grandmother, Evelyn Hansen. My grandmother was also a farmwife for many years, and as I worked on this quilt I thought of all the warm memories I had of her. She was an interesting woman who loved to hoard fabric, so it's no surprise that I would also love fabrics! She let me spend many an hour at her sewing machine making doll clothes to my heart's content, and for that reason I will always have fond memories of her. The center block is a pattern called Thrifty Housewife, which I thought was an appropriate way to start this quilt.

What You Will Need

Yardage is based on 42"-wide fabric unless otherwise noted.

Twin-size flat sheet: for foundation piecing

60" denim: 1¾ yards for backing

6 red prints: ½ yard of each for crazy piecing

6 purple prints: ¾ yard of each for crazy piecing

6 mauve/pink prints: ¾ yard of each for crazy piecing

60"-wide floral denim: ¼ yard for accent borders

60"-wide plaid denim: ½ yard for accent borders

60"-wide checked denim: ½ yard for binding

Flannel twin-size flat sheet: for batting

Repositionable basting spray: such as Sulky KK 2000

 Note

Remember to prewash all fabrics before starting. When purchasing the denim, make sure it is all cotton; stretch denim would be very hard to work with and might pucker.

Cutting

All measurements include ¼" seam allowance. Copy Thrifty Housewife block patterns A and B (pages 80 and 81) at 100%.

Sheet:

Cut 4 squares 6½" × 6½".

Cut 1 strip 4¾" × 15".

Cut 2 strips 4¾" × 19¼".

Cut 1 strip 4¾" × 23½".

Cut 1 strip 4¾" × 25½".

Cut 2 strips 4¾" × 29¾".

Cut 1 strip 4¾" × 34".

Cut 1 strip 4¾" × 36".

Cut 2 strips 4¾" × 40¼".

Cut 1 strip 4¾" × 44½".

Cut 1 strip 4¾" × 46½".

Cut 2 strips 4¾" × 50¾".

Cut 1 strip 4¾" × 55".

Floral denim:

Cut 4 strips 1½" × 15".

Cut 4 strips 1½" × 36".

Plaid denim:

Cut 4 strips 1½" × 25½".

Cut 4 strips 1½" × 46½".

Cut 1 circle, using Thrifty Housewife template A.

Backing fabric:

Cut 1 square 59" × 59".

Checked denim:

Cut strips for the binding method of your choice.

Thrifty Housewife Block

Begin by piecing the Thrifty Housewife block, composed of 4 squares 6½" × 6½" that are pieced separately and joined together to form the block. This block is the quilt center.

1. Lay a sheet 6½" × 6½" square on top of Thrifty Housewife template B, and using a fine-tip marker, mark the 4 diagonal lines. Mark 4 squares.

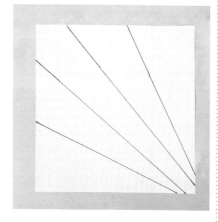

2. Refer to Flip and Sew (page 13) to piece the blocks, using an assortment of the prints. The 4 pieced squares make up the Thrifty Housewife block.

Attaching the Thrifty Housewife Block

> ### Note
> This quilt is pieced directly to the denim/flannel backing as you go. For more instructions refer to Piecing Directly onto Backing (page 26).

Thrifty Housewife block

1. Lay the 59" × 59" backing square, wrong side up, on a large surface and smooth it out. Lay the flannel sheet on top of the backing fabric and cut it to the size of the backing fabric. Follow the manufacturer's instructions for the basting spray to adhere the flannel to the denim.

2. Find the center of the denim/flannel layer and draw horizontal and vertical lines that are perpendicular to each other and cross over in the center. They should extend 7" on each side of the center.

3. Refer to the picture of a completed Thrifty Housewife block for the correct placement of the 4 squares. Lay the appropriate pieced 6½" square in the upper left quadrant that was formed when you drew the lines in the previous step. Overlap the block ¼" over the line on the right-hand side and the bottom.

4. Place another 6½" block, right sides together, on top of the first block. Pin through all layers on the right-hand side of the blocks and sew a ¼" seam allowance through all layers.

5. Flip the top block over to the right side and press the seam open.

6. Apart from the backing, sew the 2 remaining 6½" blocks together along their common edges, using a ¼" seam allowance. Flip the blocks open and press the seam.

7. Returning to the backing, lay these blocks, right sides together, on top of the first 2 blocks, lining up the bottom edge of the top blocks with the top edge of the blocks you have just sewn together. Double check the orientation of the blocks.

8. Pin in place along the lower edge through all the layers, carefully matching the seam allowance.

9. Sew with a ¼" seam allowance through all layers. Fold the top blocks open and press the seam. Check that you have placed all the blocks in the correct positions.

10. On an ironing surface lay the cut circle of plaid denim wrong side up. Press the raw edge under ¼" all the way around.

11. Pin the denim circle in the center of the Thrifty Housewife block and appliqué into place. Pin the outer edges of the blocks to the backing, making sure the flannel and denim are smoothed out.

Piecing the Crazy-Quilt Strips

Refer to Crazy Piecing Long Borders (page 17) to piece the border strips.

1. Crazy piece the following 4¾" strips you cut from the sheet, using the 6 purple fabrics: 1 strip 15", 2 strips 19¼", 1 strip 23½", 1 strip 36", 2 strips 40¼", and 1 strip 44½".

2. Crazy piece the following 4¾" strips you cut from the sheet, using the 6 red fabrics: 1 strip 25½", 2 strips 29¾", and 1 strip 34".

3. Crazy piece the following 4¾" strips you cut from the sheet, using the using 6 mauve/pink fabrics: 1 strip 46½", 2 strips 50¾", and 1 strip 55".

Adding the Sashing and Crazy Strips

Refer to Piecing Directly onto Backing (page 26). All of the piecing of the blue borders and crazy-quilted strips starts at the top of the Thrifty Housewife block (already attached to the backing). You'll add the pieces working clockwise. All the denim border strips and crazy-quilt strips have been made longer than actually needed, so you won't have to worry about exact piecing.

1. Pin a 1½" × 15" floral denim border piece, right sides together, on the top edge of the Thrifty Housewife block, extending the extra fabric evenly on both sides of the block.

2. Sew a ¼" seam allowance through all layers. Turn the denim to the right side and press in place. Pin the outer edge of the border to the quilt.

3. Repeat Steps 1 and 2 for the remaining 3 sides, working clockwise.

> **Tip**
>
> It is important that you use a clear grid ruler to square up the corners when sewing together the rest of the quilt. See the tip on squaring up (page 27).

4. Pin the purple crazy pieced 4¾" × 15" strip through all layers, right sides together, on top of the first border you sewed into place, extending the extra fabric evenly on both sides. Sew a ¼" seam allowance through all layers. Turn the purple strip to the right side and press into place. Pin the outer edge, making sure the denim/flannel is smooth underneath.

5. Add the purple crazy pieced 4¾" × 19¼" strip (right-hand side), 4¾" × 19¼" strip (bottom), and 4¾" × 23½" strip (left side) using the same process.

6. Repeat Steps 1 and 2 to add the plaid denim 1½" × 25½" border strips.

7. Add the red crazy pieced strips into place in the same way you added the purple strips: 4¾" × 25½" (top), 4¾" × 29¾" strips (right-hand side and bottom), and 4¾" × 34" strip (left side).

Gladys Kurr

Photo: Darla Osborn

8. Repeat Steps 1 and 2 to sew the floral denim 1½″ × 36″ border strips into place.

9. Sew the purple crazy pieced strips into place in the same manner as you have done all of the previous strips, starting at the top and working clockwise in this order: 4¾″ × 36″ strip (top), 4¾″ × 40¼″ strips (right-hand side and bottom), and 4¾″ × 44½″ strip (left side).

10. Repeat Steps 1 and 2 to sew the plaid denim 1½″ × 46½″ borders into place.

11. Sew the mauve/pink crazy pieced strips into place in the same manner as all of the previous strips: 4¾″ × 46½″ strip (top), 4¾″ × 50¾″ strips (right-hand side and bottom), and 4¾″ × 55″ strip (left side).

12. Because you have sewn all the pieces directly to the batting and backing, all you have left to do is trim the excess fabric around outer edges, square up the quilt, and bind it.

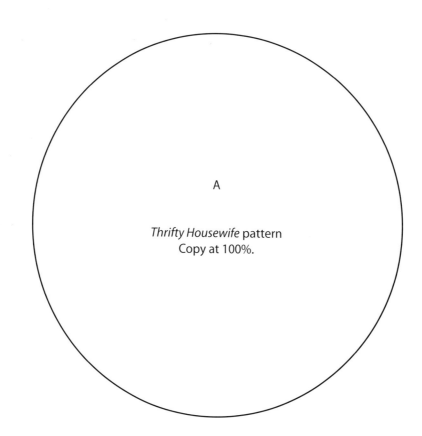

A

Thrifty Housewife pattern
Copy at 100%.

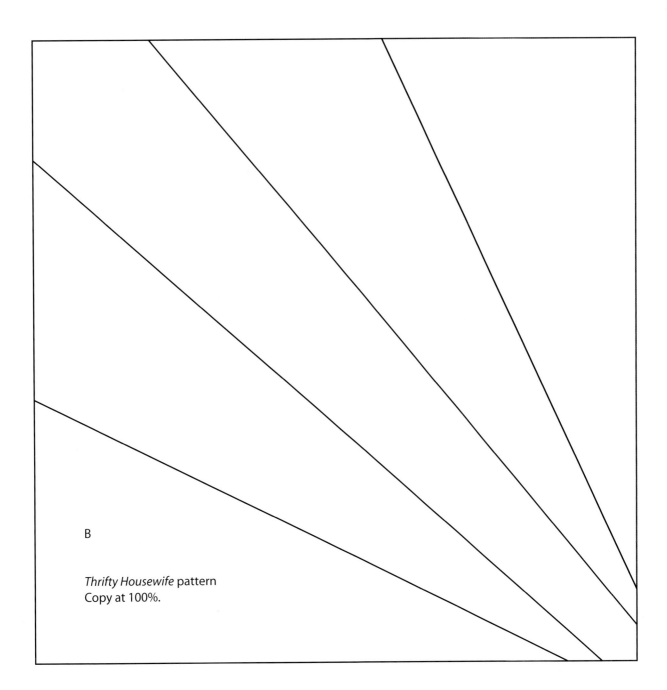

B

Thrifty Housewife pattern
Copy at 100%.

Morning Chores

Finished size: 73" × 79"

Morning Chores by Allison Aller, 2012

I used to be a dairy farmer. This quilt is a tribute to that chapter in my life and the fresh blue mornings when I would lie in bed those extra few moments before heading down to the barn. I miss those cows!

Allie feeding the cows, circa 1985

This quilt has so many nostalgic elements: vintage blocks and feed sacks; fabrics, clothing, and laces; a cut-up linen tablecloth with hand-done cross-stitch motifs; as well as some contemporary reproduction quilt cottons and ribbon. Yet all the seam embroidery and quilting are done by machine.

The following directions are for this specific quilt, but please keep in mind that *your* quilt will be unique, determined by your own collection of fabrics, blocks, laces, ribbons, and so on.

What You Will Need

Yardage is based on 42"-wide fabric unless otherwise noted.

- **10 unfinished pieced blocks:** 6½" × 6½"*
- **Printed center panel:** 19" × 25"*
- **Muslin:** 4 yards for block and strip foundations
- **White, blue, tan, and pink scraps of light value:** 3½ yards for crazy piecing**
- **Blue scraps of medium value:** 1¼ yards for crazy piecing
- **Large floral print:** 1¼ yards for inner border
- **Blue stripe:** ¼ yard, to coordinate with blue scraps
- **60"-wide denim:** 5 yards for backing and outer border
- **1 queen-size flannel sheet:** (90" × 102") for batting
- **Thin cotton batting:** 19" × 25"
- **20"-wide fusible knit interfacing:** 10 yards for foundation pieces
- **⅝"-wide pink ribbon:** 11 yards
- **½"-wide blue ribbon:** 5½ yards
- **1⅝"-wide cotton crocheted lace:** 12½ yards
- **Machine-weight threads:** in various colors for embroidering the blocks
- **12-weight pink machine embroidery thread:** for embroidering the dark denim border
- **Temporary fabric spray adhesive:** such as Sulky KK 2000

* I found a dairy feed sack and vintage blue blocks at an estate sale and planned this quilt around my treasured finds. You can piece your own 6½" × 6½" unfinished blocks for this project, using any pattern of your choice as long as you end up with 6½" × 6½" unfinished blocks.

** I included scraps from feed sacks, clothing, and laces; a cut-up linen tablecloth with hand-done cross-stitch motifs; as well as some contemporary reproduction quilt cottons and ribbon.

Cutting

*All measurements include
¼" seam allowances.*

Muslin:

Cut 12 squares 14" × 14".

Cut 6 rectangles 14" × 15½".

Cut 2 strips 6½" × 30½".

Cut 2 strips 6½" × 25".

Interfacing:

Cut 12 squares 14" × 14".

Cut 6 rectangles 14" × 15½".

Cut 2 strips 6½" × 42½".

Cut 2 strips 6½" × 36½".

Cut 2 strips 6½" × 30½".

Cut 2 strips 6½" × 25".

Blue stripe:

Cut 16 strips 1½" × 6½".

Large floral print:

(Cut from *length* of fabric.)

Cut 2 strips 6½" × 42½".

Cut 2 strips 6½" × 36½".

Denim:

(Cut from *length* of fabric.)

Cut 2 strips 4" × 84".

Cut 2 strips 4" × 90".

Fusing the Interfacings

1. Following the manufacturer's instructions, fuse all the muslin pieces with their corresponding size interfacing pieces. These are the foundations for the crazy blocks and vintage border sections.

2. Fuse the remaining 4 interfacing pieces to the corresponding 4 floral print strips. The reason for fusing these is that they need to be the same weight as the adjacent crazy blocks and vintage border in the quilt, which will have multiple layers of fabrics. This step ensures a stable and cohesive quilt top.

Quilt Layout

The quilt will be constructed section by section. Letters in the construction steps correspond with letters in the quilt layout so you can identify the sections easily.

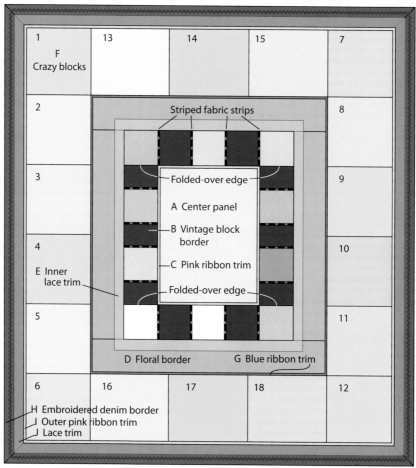

Quilt layout

Quilting the Center Panel

Refer to center panel (A) on the quilt layout.

1. Follow the manufacturer's instructions for the fabric adhesive spray. In a well-ventilated room, spray the back of the central 19″ × 25″ panel with the temporary fabric adhesive and smooth it over the thin cotton batting.

2. Machine quilt as desired.

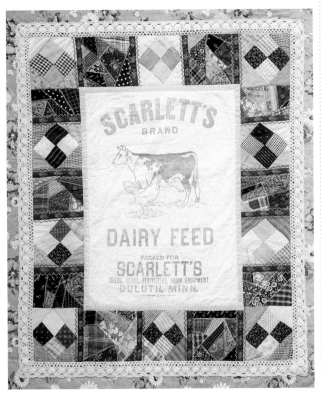

Detail of the quilted center section

3. Trim the quilted panel to 18½″ × 24½″ and machine baste ⅛″ from the edge around the panel.

Making the Vintage Block Border

Refer to vintage block border (B) on the quilt layout.

1. On the 6½″ × 30½″ foundation strips, position a 6½″ × 6½″ vintage block on the ends and a vintage block centered in the middle of the strip, placing the wrong side

of the block against the muslin side of the foundation. Machine baste ⅛″ from the edges to sew the vintage blocks into place.

2. On the 6½″ × 25″ foundation pieces, draw a line 4″ from each end. Place a 6½″ × 6½″ vintage block along the inside of each line, so the blocks are evenly spaced on the side strips. Baste into place as in Step 1.

3. On the border strips from Steps 1 and 2, use the technique in Free-Form Appliqué (page 9) to fill in the spaces next to the blocks with the assortment of medium blue scraps. Use monofilament thread to zigzag the patches in place. Refer to Pain-Free Sewing with Invisible Thread (page 10) for tips on using this thread. It's all right to leave about a ½″ muslin gap between the appliqué pieces and the raw edges of the vintage blocks. You will cover the gaps later.

The blue scraps are cut roughly and laid out between the vintage blocks.

The edges of the patches are folded under and pinned, and the machine appliqué is started, using clear thread in a zigzag stitch.

4. Use a machine stitch similar to a cross-stitch to embroider between all the blue patches of the appliquéd spaces on all the border strips.

Appliqué and embroider the blue patches.

5. Using the 1½″ × 6½″ strips of blue striped fabric, turn and press under ⅜″ on each long side, making the strips ¾″ wide.

6. On each border strip, pin the ironed strips to cover the muslin gap between the vintage blocks and the appliquéd area. Appliqué the strips in place using a zigzag stitch and clear thread. Refer to Pain-Free Sewing with Invisible Thread (page 10).

Iron, pin, and appliqué the strips into place.

7. Choose a decorative machine stitch similar to a cross-stitch and embroider along each side of all the appliquéd strips on the border strips.

Then embroider on each side of the strip.

8. Iron all 4 border strips flat from the back, and trim the edges even with the foundation.

Attaching the Vintage Block Border

1. Mark the center of each vintage block strip. Mark the center on each side of the center panel.

2. On a flat surface, lay the 6½″ × 30½″ vintage block strips along the top and bottom edges of the center section, matching the center marks and overlapping the center panel by ¼″. The corner blocks will all extend past the center section at this point. Machine baste the border strips to the center panel.

3. Fold under ½″ on the short ends of the 6½″ × 25″ vintage block strips and pin into place on each side of the center panel, again matching the centers and overlapping by ¼″. Refer to the quilt layout (page 84). Also overlap the folded-under short ends ¼″ over the corner blocks on the top and bottom block borders, and pin. With these borders around the center panel, the unit measures 30½″ × 36½″.

4. Machine appliqué the folded-under ends with clear thread in a zigzag stitch. Machine baste the side vintage block strips into place along the center panel.

5. Mark the centers of the top, side, and bottom borders.

Adding the Pink Ribbon Trim

Refer to pink ribbon trim (C) on the quilt layout.

1. Cover the raw edges of the vintage block borders where they overlap the center section by laying out the pink ribbon trim, folding a miter at the corners, and pinning all into place. Use a ruler to ensure that the corners are square.

2. Appliqué both sides of the ribbon with clear thread in a zigzag stitch. Then go back and stitch down the mitered corners.

Attaching the Floral Border and Inner Lace Trim

Refer to floral border (D) and inner lace trim (E) on the quilt layout.

1. Press under ¼″ along a long edge of the 6½″ × 36½″ floral strips. Mark the center of each strip along the folded edge. With the folded edge against the center, pin these strips to the sides of the quilt center, matching the centers.

2. Appliqué the side borders in place between the border and the quilt center, using clear thread in a zigzag stitch.

3. Repeat Steps 1–2 using the 6½″ × 42½″ floral strips for the top and bottom floral borders. With these borders around the quilt center, the unit measures 42½″ × 48½″.

4. Pin the lace trim over the seam between the vintage block border and the floral border, folding and mitering the corners. (Use a ruler to make sure they are square.)

5. Machine appliqué the lace all the way around each side, using clear thread in a zigzag stitch. Then go back and stitch down the mitered corners.

Corner detail with the mitered pink ribbon trim (C) and the inner lace trim (E)

Making the Crazy Block Border

Refer to crazy blocks 1–18 (F) on the quilt layout.

1. Use the 12 foundation squares 14″ × 14″; the 6 foundation rectangles 14″ × 15½″; and the 3½ yards of white, blue, tan, and pink scraps of light value to construct crazy patch blocks 1–18. Refer to the method in Free-Form Appliqué (page 9). Place the patches on the muslin side of the foundations. Follow the tips below for the blocks.

2. Trim blocks 1–12 to 12½″ × 12½″.

3. Trim blocks 13–18 to 12½″ × 14½″.

4. Sew around the perimeter of each trimmed block ⅛″ in from the trimmed edge.

 Tips

● Number the blocks in the upper left corner, on the interfacing side of each foundation. Keep track of blocks 13–18 because they will finish 2″ wider than the other 12 blocks.

● The foundations are cut oversize for trimming to size later. I've found that "insurance" to be necessary.

● To include cross-stitched motifs, sky fabric, and blue cherry feedsack in each block, I pinned all the muslin foundations on a design wall. Then I pinned the elements into place, balancing them among the blocks before constructing each block. Study the quilt photo (page 82) again to see what I mean.

● Keep your lace collection handy so you can appliqué it into the block as you go, rather than after the fabrics are all sewn down. Make sure the lace is sewn right side up.

● Layer large lace pieces over solid fabric before cutting and appliquéing as a single unit.

● Keep a stitch sampler handy. Refer to Crazy-Quilt Machine Embroidery Stitching (page 43) for trying out threads and stitches before you commit to embroidering them on the block.

● The machine embroidery along the seams should be simple and light. Remember not to sew too fast.

● You don't have to finish one block before starting another. Work on many blocks simultaneously, adding a few patches to one, then to another. I use a design wall so I can work on all of them all at once, composing the quilt as a whole as I do so.

● With all these thoughts in mind, go for it! Lay out, appliqué, and embroider.

With supplies at hand, a block is all pinned and ready to machine appliqué. See how lace is layered over solid fabric in a corner patch? Notice the way the narrow laces have been pinned into place as the block is laid out, not afterward. A stitch sampler is on hand, as always, for trying out stitches before committing to them in the block.

Attaching the Crazy Block Border and Blue Ribbon Trim

Refer to crazy blocks 1–18 (F) and blue ribbon trim (G) on the quilt layout.

1. Mark the ¼" sewing lines on the back of each block, if desired. I've found that marked lines help me sew these often bumpy seams more accurately.

2. Sew blocks 13, 14, and 15 together. Press the seams open. Pin this row of blocks to the top floral border, right sides together, and sew. Press the seam open.

3. Repeat Step 2 for blocks 16, 17, and 18, and sew to the bottom floral border.

4. Repeat Step 2 for blocks 1–6 and blocks 7–12, sewing each row to the sides of the quilt.

5. Lay out the blue ribbon trim over the seam between the floral and crazy block borders, folding a miter at the corners and pinning all into place. Use a ruler to ensure that the corners are square.

6. Appliqué both sides of the ribbon with clear thread in a zigzag stitch. Then go back and stitch down the mitered corners.

Making the Denim Border and Adding the Trims

Refer to embroidered denim border (H), outer pink ribbon trim (I), and lace trim (J) on the quilt layout.

1. Select the same stitch you used along the striped fabric strips in the vintage border. Using 12-weight pink embroidery thread, embroider this stitch 1" in from the edge of each 4" denim strip. Start with a full bobbin and a new jeans or topstitching needle.

2. With the embroidery toward the outside, match the center of each 4" × 84" denim strip to the top or bottom of the quilt center and pin in place with right sides together. Repeat with the 4" × 90" denim strips for the sides. Stitch in place and press these seams open from the back.

3. Miter the corners, cutting off any excess length.

4. Add the outer pink ribbon and lace trims as you did in Attaching the Crazy Block Border and Blue Ribbon Trim, Steps 5 and 6 (at left).

A finished corner

Quilting and Finishing

1. From the remaining denim backing, cut 2 pieces 2¼ yards in length and remove the selvages. Sew the pieces together along the long edges to create the quilt backing. Press the seam open. Trim the backing to 81" × 87".

2. Layer the quilt backing, right side down; the flannel sheet; and the quilt top, right side up. Pin baste the layers together, if you are quilting this yourself.

3. Mark the floral border with the quilting design of your choice.

4. Quilt in-the-ditch around all sashing and between all blocks in the inner block border and outer block border. Because my vintage blocks in the inner block border were puffy, I chose to quilt them in-the-ditch as well. I did not quilt within the crazy border blocks.

5. Quilt within the floral border on the marked lines.

6. Trim the quilt so the layers are an even ½" beyond the outer edge of the embroidery on the denim border.

7. Finish with the technique in Folded-In-and-Stitched Edge (page 28). Mark a line ½" from the edge of the denim border, all the way around the quilt. Using the line as a guide, turn the edge in toward the center of the quilt sandwich and press. Fold the batting and backing in toward the center of the quilt sandwich to match the folded edge of the denim border. Pin these folded layers together all around the quilt. Sew along the edge with a zigzag stitch in clear thread.

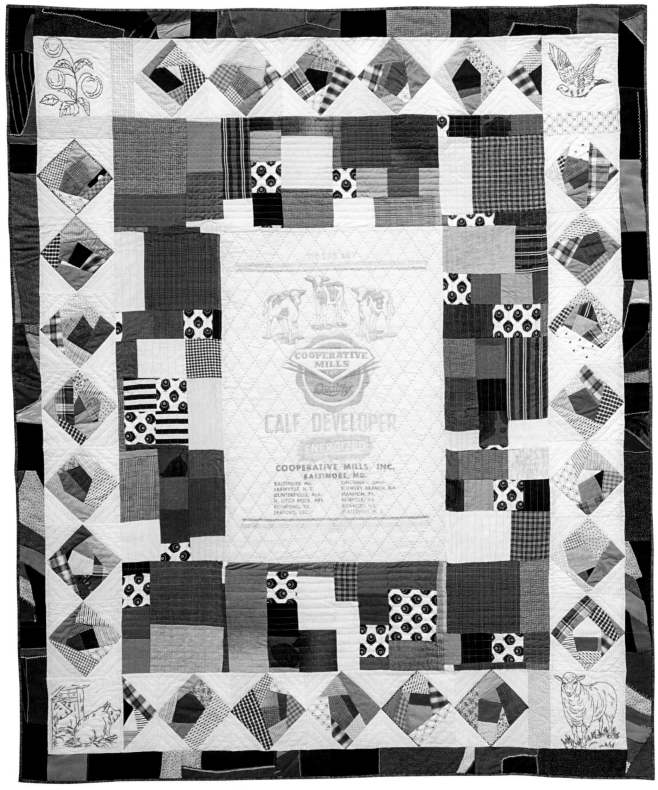

Fresh off the Farm by Victoria Findlay Wolfe, 71″ × 82″, 2013
Our friend Victoria made her own distinctly modern version of a workingman's quilt. She says, "The quilt is totally 100% repurposed from my own shirtings, fabrics I got from a friend's farm where there were boxes of work clothes already cut up in the basement, and blocks I had from eBay that were orphans from work clothes. The cream setting fabric was actually the back of a calf developer feed bag."

Fan-tastic Crazy

The gentle curves created by fans add an elegance that is visually appealing. We each used wholecloth construction, appliquéing our work to a single foundation. But beyond that, our styles and techniques greatly diverged. Val's is a delicate and serene wallhanging that has been hand embroidered in the traditional Victorian style. Allie's is a functional throw quilt made of silks and cotton velveteen, utilizing many trims with a contemporary flavor.

Val

Oriental Garden

Finished size: 28″ × 28″

Oriental Garden by Valerie Bothell, 2012

Fans are one of my favorite designs to incorporate into a quilt, and I find that they sneak their way into almost every crazy quilt I make. They can take a little bit of time to piece but are worth the extra effort in the end. This piecing method is one I have been using for many years. I find it the easiest way to piece fans onto a wholecloth quilt.

What You Will Need

Yardage is based on 42"-wide fabric unless otherwise noted.

54"-wide drapery lining: 1 yard for foundations

Burgundy silk: 1 yard for piecing and binding

Mauve print, blue silk, teal moiré, and brown silk: ⅓ yard each

Teal butterfly drapery fabric: (or any other teal fabric with a motif you like) ½ yard

Backing: 1 yard

Thin cotton batting: 32" × 32" piece

20"-wide fusible knit interfacing: ¼ yard

Burgundy lace: 2 yards

Gold metallic trim: 2 yards

Embroidery thread: in coordinating colors in silk, cotton, and metallic

Beads for embellishment

Oriental-themed charms

Air-erasable marking pen

Cutting

All measurements include ¼" seam allowances. Copy the Oriental Garden fan blade, fan top, fan bottom, and faux fan patterns (page 96 and 97) at the size indicated on each pattern piece. Use cardstock to make templates. Add the markings to each template.

Drapery lining:

    Cut 1 square 20" × 20".

    Cut 4 strips 4¼" × 21".

Teal moiré:

    Cut 4 squares 4¼" × 4¼".

    Cut 4 pieces using the fan blade template.*

Burgundy silk:

    Cut 2 strips 1" × 20".

    Cut 2 strips 1" × 21".

    Cut 4 pieces using the fan blade template.*

    Cut strips for the binding method of your choice.

Mauve print and blue silk:

    Cut 4 pieces from each color using the fan blade template.*

Interfacing:

    Cut 4 squares 4¼" × 4¼".

* Cut on the outside lines of this template as seam allowances are already included.

Making the Center Block

1. Lay out the 20" × 20" drapery lining square and mark where the fans will go by placing the fan top template in each of the 4 corners, lining up the straight edges of the template with the straight edges of the fabric. Use a permanent marker and make sure that you can also see the mark on the back of the fabric.

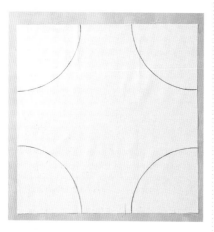

2. Using patches of burgundy, mauve, blue, teal, and brown, piece the center section of the 20" drapery lining square using the Montano Centerpiece Method (page 14), placing the butterfly or motif of your choice in the center. Piece past the lines you have drawn for the fans (later you can trim them) so the piecing overlaps the fan lines by ½".

Making the Center Corner Fans

1. Use the fan bottom template to cut out 4 pieces from the brown silk, *cutting right on the straight lines of the template but cutting the curved edge ½" beyond the curved edge of the template.*

2. Pin a brown silk fan bottom piece onto each corner of the square foundation as shown. Then use the fan bottom template to mark the curved edge and hash marks. (I usually use an air-erasable pen for this, but the illustration shows a different colored pencil for demonstration purposes.)

3. Lay the fan top template in place again and mark the curved edge and hash marks on the pieced center section as shown.

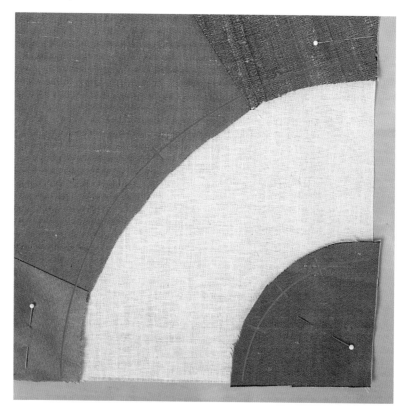

 Tip

Before piecing the fan blades, lay out all of them in the four corners of the block and move them around until you like the way they look. The fans don't have to have their fabrics all in the same order; in fact you will get better color play if you don't piece them all the same.

4. As shown, lay a fan blade piece right side up and even with the edge of the foundation and the ends of the blade, overlapping the pieced center and the brown fan bottom. Then turn under the raw edges on both ends of the fan blade so that they are even with the marked lines *only at the outside edges of the foundation*, and pin into place. (Only the outside edges of the blade are folded even with the lines of the pieced center and the brown fan bottom. After all the blades are sewn together, all the ends will be folded in and appliquéd in place.)

 Tip

If some of the fabrics you are using are a bit stretchy, line them with fusible knit interfacing to make piecing the fans easier.

5. Sew the fan blade in place on the foundation by stitching ⅛″ from the foundation raw edge.

6. Lay the next fabric fan blade wrong side up on top of the previous fan blade, lining up the raw edges. Sew a ¼″ seam between the marked lines of the fan top and bottom. Fold the fan blade over to the right side and press the seam open.

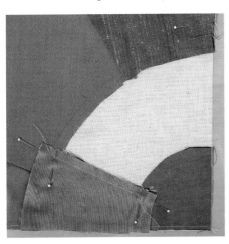

 Tip

I like to put a pin in place where my hash marks are at each end of the blade just to make sure that I am sewing the fan blade in the correct position.

7. Continue in the same manner to piece the third and fourth blades of the fan.

8. To secure the fourth blade on the outer edge of the fan, repeat what you did to the first fan blade by turning under the raw edges on both ends of the fan blade to meet the marked lines, pinning into place, and sewing to the foundation ⅛″ from the raw edge.

9. Make fans for the remaining 3 corners of the block.

10. Turn the block to the wrong side and press well. Trim any excess fabric and sew a ⅛″ basting stitch along the outside edge in any places that you may have missed.

11. Turn the pieced block to the wrong side. You should be able to see the marked line you made for the top of the fan. Place the fan bottom template into each of the 4 corners and mark the curved line. Begin to tie off the loose threads left from sewing the fans. Pull out any stitches that are closer to the marked template lines than ¼″, and then pull the second thread to the back and tie a knot.

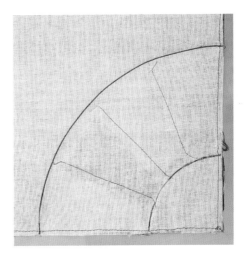

12. Once you have tied off all the loose threads for all 4 fans, you are ready to fold the raw edges of the blades under. Turn the pieced block back to the right side and choose which fan you want to work on. Fold and appliqué the top and bottom raw edges under, using the lines you marked with the templates as a guide.

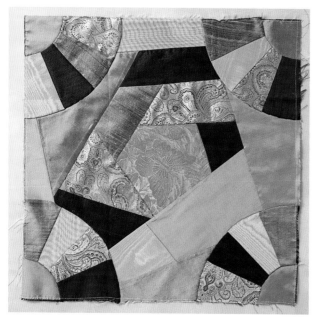

Completed block before embellishing

13. Embroider and embellish the block using crazy-quilt stitches found in Stitching and Embellishing (page 32). Have fun with it and experiment by using different combinations of the stitches. Incorporating silk ribbon embroidery is a fun way to embellish a block quickly. Use the lace and metallic trim you purchased to embellish the top of each fan.

Making the Border Strips

1. Using the remaining fabrics, cut rectangular shapes that measure 4¼" long and vary in width from 2½" to 4½". There are 4 drapery lining 4¼" × 21" foundation strips to piece, and depending on how big you cut the rectangles, you will need 7 or 8 rectangles per border.

2. Before piecing the border strips, lay the pieces out around the finished center block and move the colors around until you like the way they look. Cut more rectangles if needed.

3. Take a 4¼" × 21" drapery lining foundation strip and lay the first rectangle on the left side of the strip, right side up. Take a second rectangle and lay it on the first rectangle, right sides together. Sew a ¼" seam through all layers. Fold the second rectangle to the right side and press in place.

4. Continue piecing in this manner until you have finished piecing the strip. Turn the border to the wrong side and trim any excess fabric even with the foundation piece. Press well and sew a ⅛" basting stitch all the way around the finished border. Make 4.

5. Embroider all the border pieces so they complement the center block.

Making the Faux Corner Fans

1. Mark a fan shape with a purple air-erasable pen on each of the teal 4¼" squares using the faux fan template.

2. Stitch the lace and trim left from the center corner fans in place along the curved fan shape on each of the 4¼" squares.

3. Following the manufacturer's instructions, fuse a 4¼" interfacing square on the back of each of the teal squares.

Pieced border

Assembling and Finishing

Refer to the quilt photo (page 90) to see the borders.

1. To add the accent border, sew the 1″ × 20″ burgundy strips to the sides of the quilt center with right sides together. Flip the accent borders to the right side, and press the seams toward the burgundy strips.

2. Sew the 1″ × 21″ burgundy strips to the top and bottom of the quilt center, rights sides together. Flip the accent borders to the right side, and press the seams toward the burgundy strips.

3. Pin and sew pieced 4¼″ × 21″ border strips to opposite sides of the quilt center. Press toward the burgundy border.

4. Sew a teal faux fan square to each end of the remaining pieced border strips, positioning the fans correctly. Refer to the quilt photo (page 90). Press the seams toward the squares.

5. Add these border pieces to the quilt center and press the seams toward the burgundy border.

6. Layer the backing, batting, and quilt top. Inside tie the wallhanging, referring to Interior Tying Method (page 24).

7. Bind the quilt with the burgundy silk, using the binding method of your choice.

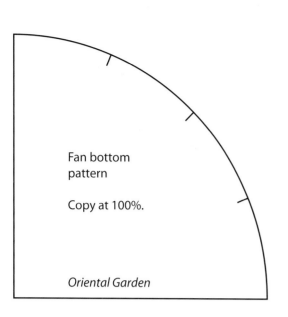

Fan bottom
pattern

Copy at 100%.

Oriental Garden

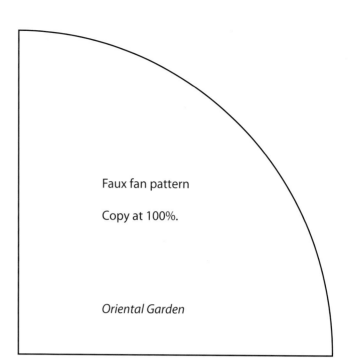

Faux fan pattern

Copy at 100%.

Oriental Garden

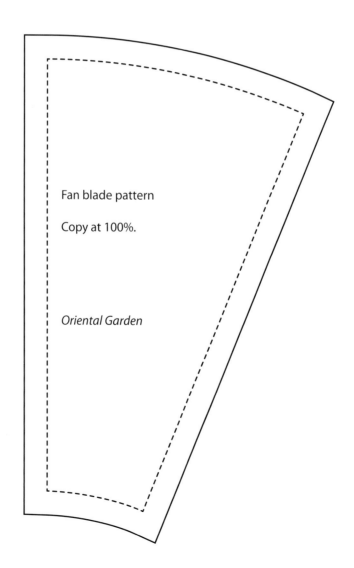

Fan blade pattern

Copy at 100%.

Oriental Garden

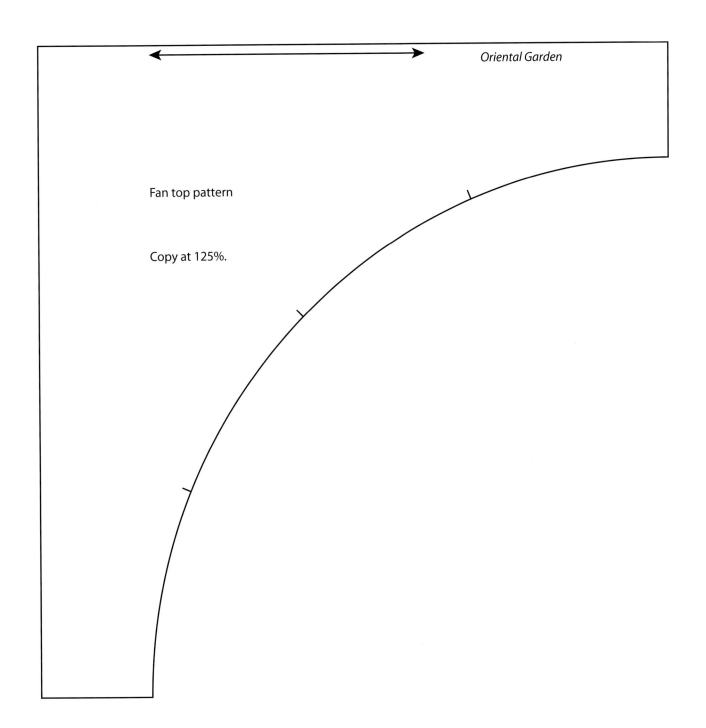

Oriental Garden

Fan top pattern

Copy at 125%.

Color Block Fans

Finished size: 58″ × 71″

Color Block Fans by Allison Aller, 2013

This quilt has an unusual construction, so let's examine how it is put together before we get started …

The fabric "blades" are cut out using templates and machine basted onto a muslin foundation. Strips of trim are then machine appliquéd over the adjacent raw edges of the blades. The quarter-circle base is also machine basted into place, covering the bottom edges of the fabric blades and trims, with its raw edge later covered by ribbon embroidery. One side of each length of trim on each block throughout the entire quilt is also embroidered.

The completed blocks are laid out on a wholecloth background. (For some different block layout ideas, see Block Settings and Border Arrangements, page 18.) They are then raw-edge appliquéd in place, leaving sections of the background uncovered. Those sections become part of the quilt's composition—in this case, the large purple triangles. More strips of ribbon then cover the raw edges between and around the blocks, and around the perimeter of the quilt. Ribbons, ribbons, ribbons! I've simplified the materials list with fewer ribbons than I used, but there is still plenty of variety.

What You Will Need

Yardage is based on 42″-wide fabric unless otherwise noted.

FOR THE BLOCKS

Muslin: 2 yards for foundations

20″-wide fusible knit interfacing: 4½ yards

Warm-colored silk scraps: 2 yards

Cool-colored silk scraps: 1¾ yards

Pale warm-colored silk scraps: ⅓ yard

Very dark warm-colored silk scraps: ⅓ yard

⅜″- to 1″-wide assorted trims and ribbons: 40 yards

Warm-colored velvet: ¼ yard

Cool-colored velvet: ¼ yard

Scrap of pale warm-colored velvet: at least 6″ × 6″

Scrap of dark warm-colored velvet: at least 6″ × 6″

12-weight silk or perle cotton embroidery thread: assorted colors (You could also use 2 strands of silk or cotton floss in the block embroidery.)

4mm silk ribbon: assorted colors

Clear monofilament thread

Jeans or topstitching machine needle: in a medium size

Chalk marker

Tacky glue

Freezer paper

Optional: Ruler-marked masking tape (available at scrapbook supply stores)

RIBBONS

1½″ gold jacquard ribbon: 16 yards for ribbon binding

⅝″-wide printed yellow ribbon: 11½ yards for diamond perimeter and purple perimeter

⅝″-wide printed orange ribbon: 8 yards for the diamond perimeter and the top and bottom rows

½″-wide printed yellow ribbon: 6 yards for center diamond

½″-wide printed blue ribbon: 4½ yards for center diamond

½″-wide black jacquard ribbon: ⅞ yard for center diamond

BACKGROUND, BACKING, AND BATTING

60″-wide purple cotton velveteen: 2 yards for wholecloth background

Backing: 3¾ yards

Batting: 64″ × 77″ piece

Note

If you want a lighter-weight quilt, use a very thin cotton batting, or no batting at all. I used organic cotton fleece, purchased from a cloth diaper supply company, for extra warmth and stability.

 Note

I chose velveteen for the wholecloth background because it is sturdy and I love the texture of it. But of course, any fabric that strikes your fancy is fine, as long as it is not too lightweight. The heaviness of the blocks being appliquéd onto it requires some support; therefore, if you use cotton or silk for the background, I recommend interfacing it first. If you use a 42″-wide fabric, you will need 4 yards so the seam in the middle can be covered by the appliquéd blocks.

Cutting

All measurements include ¼″ seam allowances. Additional cutting will be done within the construction steps.

Warm-color velvet:

Cut 6 squares 6″ × 6″.

Cool-color velvet:

Cut 5 squares 6″ × 6″.

Pale velvet:

Cut 1 square 6″ × 6″.

Dark velvet:

Cut 1 square 6″ × 6″.

Making the Blocks

Make 24 warm, 20 cool, 4 pale, and 4 dark blocks.

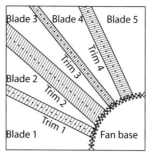

Fan block

Preparing the Fabrics and Templates

1. Trace the *Color Block Fans* blade patterns 1–5 (page 105) onto freezer paper and cut them out on the lines. Copy the fan base pattern (page 104) onto cardstock and cut it out on the lines. Mark each blade template with the blade number and mark the lines on the fan base template.

2. Following the manufacturer's instructions, fuse the interfacing to the muslin.

3. Cut 52 squares 6½″ × 6½″ from the fused muslin.

4. Fuse interfacing to the backs of all 13 velvet 6″ × 6″ squares.

Piecing the Blocks

For each block:

1. To cut out the fan bases, use the fan base template and a chalk marker to draw a 5″ circle on a prepared velvet square. (You do not want to iron the freezer paper onto the velvet because when you pull it off it will take some of the nap with it.) Then mark the circle into even quarters, drawing a line 2½″ in from the edge both horizontally and vertically. Cut out the circle, and then cut it into quarters.

2. Each block requires a set of blades 1–5, so think in blade sets. You will need 24 warm blade sets, 20 cool sets, 4 pale sets, and 4 dark sets. To make a set of warm blades, iron freezer-paper blade templates 1–5 onto silk scraps of 5 different warm colors.

3. Cut out the blades a scant ¼″ outside the edges of the template. (This will allow you to overlap the blades on the foundation.) Remove the freezer paper, but keep track of the template blade numbers for each piece. Repeat this cutting process so you have 24 warm sets, 20 cool sets, 4 pale sets, and 4 dark sets of each blade.

4. Lay out a set of blades onto a prepared muslin foundation square, overlapping the blades' inside edges and letting their outside edges extend ¼″ beyond the foundation. Pin the blades into place.

5. Using a straight stitch, sew the blades within the overlapping area between the blades.

Set of warm blades sewn to foundation

6. Choose 4 different trims to cover the inside raw, overlapped edges of the blades. Cut them to length (plus a little extra for insurance) and pin into place, covering the raw edges.

7. Carefully position the fan base on the muslin foundation, lining up the corners. Velvet is very wiggly, so it helps to glue baste it into place on the block before pinning it into place. Spread a very light coating of the tacky glue along the curved edge of the fan base, on the interfacing side, with your finger. Because the glue is spread on the interfacing, it won't show through on the velvet. Gently press the velvet raw edge down along the curve with your fingers. Then pin at 1" intervals along the curve.

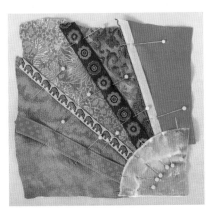

Pin trims and fan base.

8. Stitch along each side of the trims with a zigzag stitch. Refer to Pain-Free Sewing with Invisible Thread (page 10). Then stitch along the raw-edge curve of the fan base.

9. Flip the block over. Use a ruler and the edge of the interfaced foundation as a guide to trim the block to exactly 6½" × 6½". Sew a straight stitch around the perimeter of the block, ⅛" in from the edge. This will prevent the edges of the silk from unraveling as you are handling the block while embroidering it.

10. Repeat Steps 2–9 to complete 24 warm blocks, 20 cool blocks, 4 pale blocks, and 4 dark blocks, for a total of 52 blocks.

Embroidering the Blocks

1. On each block, embroider along the "down-side" edge of the trim, using the Cretan/herringbone combination stitch (page 37) with the size 12 perle cotton thread, as shown in the photo.

2. If you have the optional ruler-marked masking tape, position a piece of it parallel to the first length of trim, about ½" from the edge of the trim, using the marks on the tape to help with the spacing.

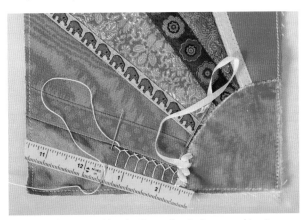

Adhesive ruler tape guides the Cretan/herringbone combination stitching. Also shown is the closely spaced herringbone stitch, done in silk ribbon along the fan base curve (Step 4).

3. Embroider along the "down-side" edge of the remaining 3 trims, switching thread colors as desired.

4. To cover the raw edge of the fan base, embroider a line of closely spaced herringbone stitches in 4mm silk ribbon. Use the silk ribbon herringbone stitch (page 40). Embroider all 52 blocks.

Completed warm block

Finishing the Quilt Top
Appliquéing the Blocks

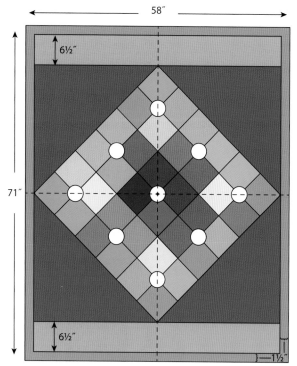

58″

6½″

71″

6½″

1½″

Maintain a 1½″ margin all around.

1. You will need a large flat surface where you can spread out the entire foundation. Remove the selvages from the velveteen, square it up to 58″ × 71″, and mark the center of all 4 sides. Refer to the block placement diagram. Lightly draw a line from side center to side center and a line from top center to bottom center. The intersection of these 2 lines is the midpoint of the velveteen foundation. Mark the side centers, top and bottom centers, and intersection point on the front and back of the foundation. On the foundation front, mark a 1½″ margin from the outside edge on all sides. At the top and bottom, draw a horizontal line 6½″ in from the 1½″ margin line.

2. Have lots of pins on hand. Referring to the quilt photo (page 98), begin arranging the center diamond blocks from the marked center point outward, starting with the 4 dark blocks. Note the positions of the fan bases as you arrange the blocks. Position the blocks with their edges butted together, and pin into place. All the raw edges will be covered with trim later.

3. Refer to the quilt photo again. Add the remaining 32 blocks to form the center diamond, positioning the warm, cool, and pale blocks in the appropriate places. As you pin them into place, check with a large ruler to make sure the lines of blocks are straight and that each point of the diamond is equidistant from the outside center to the midpoint of the foundation. The center diamond will fit inside the outside margin lines.

4. Refer to the quilt photo (page 98) for the correct block orientation for the rows across the top and bottom. Starting with the center of each row on the 6½″ line, pin 8 warm blocks into place, leaving ⅓″ space between them and ⅓″ space on each end of the row, using the marked chalk line to guide you.

5. To appliqué the blocks to the foundation, use a clear monofilament thread, a 40- to 50-weight thread in the bobbin, and a large-eyed needle (such as topstitching or jeans). I set my stitch to 4.5mm wide and 1.5mm long, but since your machine may be different, set the zigzag to catch both rows of blocks as you go.

6. Basically, you will be sewing along the diamond grid formed by the blocks. Starting along a side of the grid, stitch the edges of the blocks on a side of the diamond, removing the pins as you sew.

7. Sew the next row in on the grid, catching both rows of blocks as you sew.

8. Repeat for the remaining rows in that side of the grid. Then rotate the wholecloth foundation, and appliqué the 7 lines of the grid in the other direction. All of the central 36 blocks are now completely attached to the wholecloth foundation.

9. For the top and bottom rows of blocks, sew along the vertical sides of each block. Then sew along the entire line of blocks, first along the top and then the bottom.

Appliquéing the Ribbons

1. The ribbon placement for the diamond trims is shown here. Use the black ½"-wide, yellow ½"-wide, and blue ½"-wide ribbons for the *inside* grid of the diamond as shown by the dark black, yellow, and blue lines. Pin all the pieces of ribbon on the diamond center. In the center, you can weave the ribbons over and under each other if you wish.

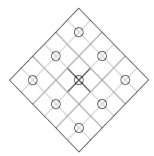

Placement of black, yellow, and blue ½"-wide ribbons

2. Appliqué along each edge of each piece of ribbon, using clear monofilament thread in a zigzag stitch, as you stitched the trim to the blocks.

3. Pin vertical orange ⅝"-wide ribbon strips into place on each end of the top and bottom rows and between the blocks. Pin the same orange ⅝"-wide ribbon around the *outside* perimeter of the diamond. You don't need to miter the ribbon at the corners of the diamond; just cut strips to overlap slightly at the diamond corners. The ends of these ribbons will be covered in Step 6.

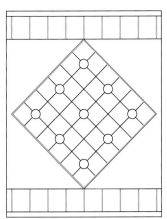

Placement of orange ribbons

4. Sew the orange ribbon strips into place, as in Step 2.

5. Use a ruler and the chalk to mark a vertical line along each side of the quilt between the ends of the top and bottom rows. Each line should touch a side tip of the center diamond.

6. Pin and appliqué the yellow ⅝"-wide ribbon along the bottom edge of the top row of blocks. Miter the corner and continue around the outside perimeter of the purple foundation as shown. Tuck the ribbon ends into the last corner miter. This yellow ribbon will cover the ends of the orange ribbons at the tips of the center diamond.

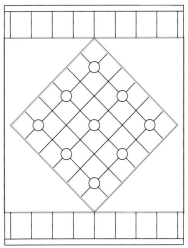

Placement of ⅝"-wide yellow ribbons for Steps 6 and 7

7. Starting at the bottom corner, pin the yellow ⅝"-wide ribbon adjacent to the orange ribbon all the way around the *inside* perimeter of the center diamond, mitering the ribbon at each corner. Hide the ribbon ends in the final miter. The mitered corners at the top and bottom tips of the diamond will be on top of the yellow ribbon from Step 6. Zigzag stitch each side of the ribbon, all the way around.

Mitered corner at top of diamond

Assembling and Finishing

Constructing the Quilt Sandwich

1. Piece the backing and trim to 64" × 77".

2. Layer the quilt backing (face down), the batting, and the quilt centered on top.

3. If you are quilting this yourself, then pin baste the layers together, spacing the safety pins 4" apart.

Quilting

To match the quilting on my *Color Block Fans* quilt, follow these steps.

1. Use a clear monofilament thread in the top and a thread in the bobbin that matches the quilt backing. Quilt in-the-ditch around all the ribbon trims on the quilt top, removing the safety pins as you go.

2. Switch to the machine quilting thread of your choice to quilt the purple triangle areas. I used simple parallel lines, but these are the areas where you dedicated machine quilting artists can quilt fancy designs to your heart's content.

Binding

For this binding, you will be sandwiching the outside edge of the quilt between 2 layers of 1½"-wide ribbon that are appliquéd around the quilt's perimeter. A ribbon is appliquéd along the front-side edges and a ribbon is pinned along the back-side edges. The outside edges of the 2 ribbons will be sewn closed all the way around the quilt to give the finished edge.

1. Trim all layers of the quilt sandwich even with the quilt top.

2. Leaving a 4" tail of ribbon at the top left corner of the quilt, begin pinning 1½"-wide ribbon along the top of the quilt front, with the ribbon overlapping the blocks ¼". Miter the corner with an accurate 90° angle, and continue pinning the ribbon down a side so that it aligns with the point of the inside ribbon trim on the diamond. Continue pinning down to the bottom row of blocks, mitering the corner and overlapping the lower edge by ¼" as you did at the top. Continue pinning the ribbon around the perimeter to the starting point. Trim the ends of the ribbon so that you tuck the raw ends into the final corner miter.

3. Zigzag the inner edge of the ribbon into place through all the layers of the quilt sandwich. Whipstitch down the ribbon miters through the ribbon only.

4. Carefully trim the quilt sandwich ⅛" inside the outer edge of the ribbon.

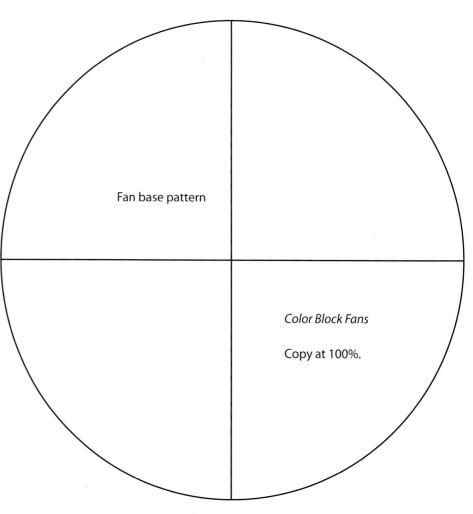

Fan base pattern

Color Block Fans

Copy at 100%.

5. Turn the quilt over. Pin a second length of the 1½″-wide ribbon around the perimeter of the back of the quilt along the outside edge of the ribbon, aligning it with the outside edge of the front ribbon.

6. Fold, miter, and pin in the corners, hiding the ends of the ribbon in the miter of the last corner. Sew the *outer* edges of the ribbons together all the way around. This is the finished edge. Then go back and whipstitch the inner edge of the ribbon to the back of the quilt. Whipstitch down the miters as you get to them.

7. Trim any loose threads off the back and front of the quilt.

Corners of the ribbon binding (front and back)

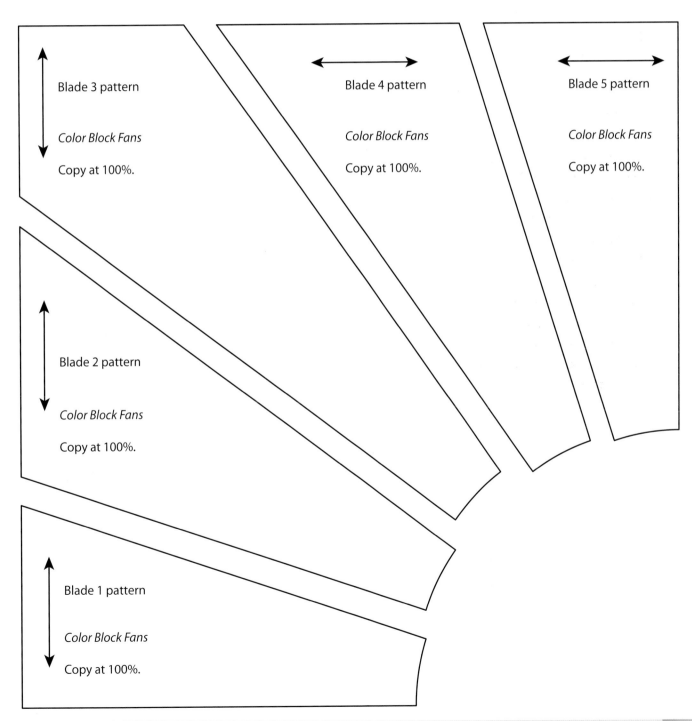

Blade 3 pattern

Color Block Fans

Copy at 100%.

Blade 4 pattern

Color Block Fans

Copy at 100%.

Blade 5 pattern

Color Block Fans

Copy at 100%.

Blade 2 pattern

Color Block Fans

Copy at 100%.

Blade 1 pattern

Color Block Fans

Copy at 100%.

Historically Crazy

My Crazy Dream by Mary M. Hernandred Ricard, 68½″ × 74″, pieced from 1877 to 1912

Photo: International Quilt Study Center

One of the best-known crazy quilts in existence is *My Crazy Dream* by Mary M. Hernandred Ricard, owned by the International Quilt Study Center in Lincoln, Nebraska. The quilt graces the cover of Penny McMorris's book *Crazy Quilts* and can be found in many other historical quilt books as well. We had the opportunity to spend a long time with this quilt in Lincoln, and it was a very moving experience. The intense—almost obsessed—stitching is like a window into Mrs. Ricard's soul. This communion with *My Crazy Dream* deeply inspired each of us. Partly as homage, and partly for the unique experience of stepping into Mrs. Ricard's very thought process as a crazy quilter, we decided to take a pieced section of the quilt and each reproduce it in our own way using modern fabrics and methods. We hope you too will take steps backward and forward in time with us and create your own "crazy dream."

Our thanks to the International Quilt Study Center for its permission to undertake this project for publication.

Photo: International Quilt Study Center

Section of *My Crazy Dream* that was reproduced

I Dream in Pink

Finished size: 28″ × 26″

I Dream in Pink by Valerie Bothell, 2012

My favorite color is pink and I just couldn't resist using it for this project! I looked through all of my fabrics and came up with a lot of pinks, from the very pale to the very bright. I paired the pinks with a lot of green, from soft greens to a lime green silk.

This project is a piecing challenge, but it is well worth the effort in the end. I used my techniques described in Cardstock Appliqué Crazy Piecing (page 11) and Flip and Sew (page 13) to construct this fanciful block. When piecing

it, take your time and enjoy the process. Embellishing a block is my favorite part of crazy quilting, but you must piece a block to have one to embellish. After piecing a challenging block such as this one, your reward will be great: a fabulous block to treasure for many years.

If pink is not your favorite color, try your own color scheme. It is always an option to enlarge or reduce the size of this pattern according to how big you want to make the block.

What You Will Need

Yardage is based on 42"-wide fabric unless otherwise noted.

- **Drapery lining fabric:** ⅝ yard for foundation
- **Lime green silk:** ½ yard
- **Variety of pink silk scraps:** ½ yard
- **Variety of green silk scraps:** ½ yard
- **Bright pink silk:** ⅝ yard for border (The border is all from the same bright pink, although the sheen makes it look like 2 different fabrics.)
- **Pale green silk:** ⅛ yard for accent border
- **Backing:** ¾ yard
- **Batting:** 30" × 32" piece
- **2"-wide jacquard trim:** 3½ yards for binding
- **20"-wide fusible knit interfacing:** 2 yards
- **Cotton print of an old postcard:** for block center*
- **Silk ribbons in various shades of pink and green:** 4mm and 7mm, for embellishment
- **Silk and metallic threads in pink and green:** for embellishment
- **Perle cotton size 8**

Optional: Variety of trims, pink and green beads, and charms

* You may not find a printed postcard, but you can select another focal point for the block.

Cutting

All measurements include ¼" seam allowance. Additional cutting will be done in the construction steps.

Drapery lining:

Cut 1 piece 19½" × 21½".

Lime green silk:

Cut 1 piece 10" × 16".

Bright pink:

Cut 2 pieces 3¾" × 26½".

Cut 2 pieces 3¾" × 22".

Pale green:

Cut 2 strips 1¼" × 20½".

Cut 2 strips 1¼" × 20".

Interfacing:

Cut 1 piece 19½" × 21½".

Cut 1 piece 10" × 16".

Cut 2 pieces 3¾" × 26½".

Cut 2 pieces 3¾" × 22".

Cut 2 strips 1¼" × 20½".

Cut 2 strips 1¼" × 20".

Backing:

Cut 1 piece 30" × 32".

Piecing the Block

This block uses two piecing techniques that have been covered in other sections of the book: Cardstock Appliqué Crazy Piecing (page 11) and Flip and Sew (page 13). Read each section completely before beginning this project. You should be familiar with the process of each technique. Except for the center lime green silk, you select the colors for the quilt pieces from the variety of pink and green scraps. You can plan ahead or plan as you go. It's up to you.

Copying the Pattern

1. Locate the *I Dream in Pink* pattern on the pullout page. This pattern is divided between the front and back of the pattern sheet, so copy both halves and tape them together. (It is always an option to enlarge or reduce the size of this pattern.)

2. Center the 21½" × 19½" piece of drapery lining on top of the pullout pattern and use a fine-tip permanent marker to trace the entire pattern onto the fabric, including the outside edges of the block. Label the fabric with the numbers. Make sure that you can see the marks on the front and back of the fabric. This is the block foundation.

3. Copy the entire pattern onto cardstock as in Cardstock Appliqué Crazy Piecing (page 11). Label each piece with its number and cut the cardstock pattern apart. These are the templates.

4. Copy onto cardstock pieces 22–25 as a single template and pieces 26–32 as a single template. Do not cut the pieces apart, but label them with the numbers. You will use these large templates in addition to the individual templates you cut for these pieces.

Preparing the Center Piece

1. Following the manufacturer's instructions, fuse the cut interfacing pieces to the coordinating border pieces and to the lime green 10″ × 16″ piece.

2. Following the cutting instructions in Cardstock Appliqué Crazy Piecing (page 11), place the center piece template, label side down, on the wrong side of the interfaced 10″ × 16″ green silk piece and cut, leaving a generous ¼″ seam allowance all the way around the shape. This is the process that you will use to cut all the pattern pieces as you progress through the steps.

Adding Pieces 1–13 to the Center Piece

If pieces are for the Flip and Sew method, use the cardstock templates to rough cut the pieces. Otherwise, cut the pieces with a ¼″ seam allowance.

1. Locate pieces 1–13 on the pattern, in the lower left corner. Starting with piece 1, use the templates to rough cut the scrap pieces for the Flip and Sew method (page 13). Beginning with piece 1, Flip and Sew pieces 1–13 to the foundation, stitching from the back side of each piece. (If the traced lines do not show well through the interfacing, draw the pattern lines on the interfacing.)

Tip
To add variety to the block, I used a piece of wide ribbon for piece 4. I appliquéd the ribbon in place after the other pieces were sewn. If you don't want to use a ribbon, you may just make piece 4 another piece of fabric that you Flip and Sew into place.

2. Sew the bottom edge of the center piece using Flip and Sew. Flip the center section to the right side of the fabric. Hand appliqué the left side of the center piece, as explained in Cardstock Appliqué Crazy Piecing (page 11).

Adding Pieces 14–33

If pieces are for the Flip and Sew method, use the cardstock templates to rough cut the pieces. Otherwise, cut the pieces with a ¼″ seam allowance.

1. Sew pieces 14 and 15 to the foundation using Flip and Sew.

2. Sew pieces 16–18 together with ¼″ seams, but do not sew to the foundation. Once they are joined as a unit, sew the unit to the foundation using Flip and Sew.

3. Use the template to press under the curved edge of piece 19. Refer to Cardstock Appliqué Crazy Piecing (page 11). Hand appliqué piece 19 on top of piece 20. Then Flip and Sew the unit along piece 13, the center section, and pieces 14, 15, and 18.

4. Flip and Sew piece 21 to pieces 19 and 20.

5. Sew pieces 22–25 together with ¼″ seams, but do not sew to the foundation. Once they are sewn together as a unit, use the large 22–25 template to press under the curved edge of the unit that will adjoin piece 21. Hand appliqué this unit to pieces 12, 13, 19, and 21, and the foundation.

6. Sew pieces 26–32 together with ¼″ seams, but do not sew to the foundation. Notice that pieces 27 and 28 must be sewn together before they are sewn into the unit. Use the large 26–32 template to press under the curved edge that will adjoin piece 21. Hand appliqué this unit to piece 21, butting the edges up against pieces 24–25. You are more than halfway to the end!

Pieces 22–25 and 26–32 sewn together, with each group treated as a single unit

Adding Pieces 33–46

If pieces are for the Flip and Sew method, use the cardstock templates to rough cut the pieces. Otherwise, cut the pieces with a ¼″ seam allowance.

1. Use template 33 to press under ¼″ on the sides that will lie against piece 34. Before sewing these to the foundation, hand appliqué piece 33 on top of piece 34. Turn under the edges of piece 34 to hand appliqué to the foundation.

2. Place pieces 35 and 36 on the foundation. Hand appliqué the lower turned edges of piece 37 onto pieces 35 and 36.

3. Flip and Sew pieces 38–41 to the foundation.

4. Sew pieces 42 and 43 together with a ¼″ seam. Hand appliqué the top of piece 43 to piece 41 on the foundation.

5. Sew pieces 44 and 45 together with a ¼″ seam. Hand appliqué the unit to the green center piece and to pieces 35 and 42.

6. Use the template on piece 46 to press under ¼″ on all edges. Hand appliqué all 3 sides to the foundation.

Adding Pieces 47–57

If pieces are for the Flip and Sew method, use the cardstock templates to rough cut the pieces. Otherwise, cut the pieces with a ¼″ seam allowance.

1. Flip and Sew piece 47 on the side that adjoins pieces 44, 35, 37, 39, and 40. Hand appliqué the long left edge and the center section edge.

2. Use the template on piece 48 to press under ¼″ on the top curved edge and 2 straight sides. Hand appliqué the pressed edges to the foundation.

3. Use the template on piece 49 to press under ¼″ on the top curved edge. Hand appliqué the curved edge to the foundation.

4. Flip and Sew piece 50 to the foundation.

5. Use the template on piece 51 to press under ¼″ on the top curved edge and the edge that joins the green center. Hand appliqué the top curved edge and the edge adjoining the green center. Repeat, using piece 52.

6. Flip and Sew piece 53 to the foundation.

7. Repeat Step 5 for piece 54.

Pink polka dot fabric is piece 54.

8. Flip and Sew pieces 55 and 56.

9. Use the template on piece 57 to press under ¼″ on the curved edge. Hand appliqué the curved edge in place.

10. Turn the completed block to the wrong side to carefully press the back. Following the manufacturer's instructions, fuse the interfacing 19½″ × 21½″ piece to the back of the block.

11. Trim the block ¼″ beyond the drawn outside border of the block. Be sure that this unit squares up to 20½″ × 18½″. Sew ⅛″ around the block edges. If you can believe it, you are done piecing this beauty!

Embellishing

Embellish to your heart's content. Use those ribbons, threads, beads, and charms! You may refer to the photo of my block (page 107) or do your own thing, but whatever you do, treasure every moment of it.

Assembling and Finishing

1. Sew the green 1¼″ × 20½″ strips to the top and bottom of the block. Press the seams toward the green sashing.

2. Sew the green 1¼″ × 20″ strips to the block sides. Press the seams toward the green sashing.

3. Sew the bright pink 3¾″ × 22″ pieces to the top and bottom of the block. Press the seams toward the green sashing.

4. Sew the bright pink 3¾″ × 26½″ pieces to the block sides. Press the seams toward the green sashing.

5. Layer the backing, batting, and quilt top together.

6. Inside tie the center block using the instructions in Interior Tying Method (page 24).

> **Tip**
>
> **After you have tied the center section but before you bind the wallhanging, you could hand quilt the borders to give it added dimension. Refer to Hand Quilting (page 42) for instructions.**

7. Bind the wallhanging using a coordinating jacquard ribbon. Refer to Trim Binding (page 29).

My Washougal Dream

Finished size: 20″ × 18″

The little yellow house in its country setting between the flowers and the stars is where I live, and where I dream …

My Washougal Dream by Allison Aller, 2013

I have radically reinterpreted Mrs. Ricard's intent with her piecing, even while retaining the exact same layout. Dividing the block in half visually by employing sky colors above and garden colors below, this becomes a large landscape crazy-quilt block. I used the Freezer-Paper Template Appliqué technique (page 7). The center scene is created on a separate muslin foundation and then cut to size, and becomes the last of all the pieces to go on. A small amount of hand embroidery is added to it, while gathered silk ribbon and trims are used to frame the scene and cover its raw edge. The embellishment of the rest of the block is done in layers: First there is machine embroidery along the seams with a small amount of hand stitching and painting added to the machine-embroidered base. The night sky is beaded with the moon and stars, and then printed flowers from quilt fabric are fussy cut and raw-edge appliquéd. Finally, three-dimensional flowers and trim (with some beading) constitute the top layer and give the garden life.

What You Will Need

Yardage is based on 42"-wide fabric unless otherwise noted. These supplies are for my project, but your dream project will no doubt be unique.

MAIN BLOCK AREA

- **Green silk fabric:** 1 yard for backing and French facing
- **Garden print and green fabrics:** 22–25 scraps 6" × 6"
- **Medium and dark blue sky fabrics:** 22–25 scraps 6" × 6"
- **Fabrics for transition between garden and sky:** 10 scraps 6" × 6"
- **Print floral and leaf fabrics:** several scraps 10" × 10" to fussy cut
- **2 sprays of cloth flowers:** (available at craft stores; you will disassemble them)
- **13mm pink silk ribbon:** 3–5 yards
- **Lacelike embroidered trim:** 1 yard
- **9–12 large green beads:** for flower centers
- **12–15 flower beads:** for flower centers
- **50–100 blue and silver 3mm, 4mm, and 8mm Swarovski bicone crystal beads:** for stars and flower centers
- **1 tube each of white, clear, silver, and blue seed beads:** (and any other starlike beads that strike your fancy)
- **1 skein of yellow cotton embroidery floss**
- **1"-diameter mother-of-pearl disk button:** for moon
- **Silver fabric paint and small brush**

Optional: Small sew-on motifs, machine-embroidered butterfly or other

CENTER SCENE

- **Various green:** 7 scraps 8" × 12" for hills
- **Gray:** 1 scrap 8" × 8" for walk and roadway
- **Blue:** 1 scrap 6" × 10" for sky
- **Very dark green:** 2 scraps 6" × 6" for trees
- **Scraps:** 8" × 8" for house, windows, bushes, and tree trunk

Frame around Center Scene

- **Fancy rayon rickrack:** ⅝ yard
- **Green wool:** 1 scrap 6" × 6" for leaves
- **13mm-wide green silk ribbon:** 3 yards
- **Green jacquard trim:** ⅜ yard
- **8–10 small premade cloth flowers**
- **8–10 flower beads**

General Supplies

- **Muslin:** 1 yard for foundations
- **20"-wide fusible knit interfacing:** 1½ yards for foundations
- **20"-wide lightweight fusible web:** ½ yard
- **Lightweight batting:** 1 piece 24" × 24" and 1 piece 16" × 16"
- **Monofilament thread**
- **40- to 50-weight thread:** for bobbin
- **Blue Nymo beading thread**
- **Machine embroidery thread:** 6–10 spools, including silver metallic thread
- **Green machine threads:** for outlining hills
- **Hand embroidery floss:** in various colors for outlining roof and doorway, and adding wildflowers
- **Beading needles**
- **Hand embroidery needles**
- **Fabric-marking tool of choice**
- **Freezer paper**
- **Temporary adhesive fabric spray**

Cutting

Muslin:

Cut 1 piece 24" × 24".

Cut 1 piece 16" × 16".

Interfacing:

Cut 1 piece 24" × 24".

Cut 1 piece 16" × 16".

Main Block Area

Preparing the Foundation and Appliquéing the Patches

1. Locate the *My Washougal Dream* background pattern (pullout pages P1 and P2). The pattern is divided between the front and the back of the pattern sheet, so copy both and tape the halves together.

2. Center the 24″ × 24″ muslin piece on top of the pattern and trace the pattern onto the muslin. Number the patches. This will help you position the patches in sequence as you appliqué them.

3. Follow the manufacturer's instructions to interface the back of the 24″ × 24″ muslin piece.

4. Trace the entire pattern on the dull side of the freezer paper, again making sure to number each patch. Cut apart the freezer-paper pattern.

> **Tip**
>
> If you have the space on your worktable, lay out the original pattern and place each cut-out template piece over its corresponding space on the pattern. It will help you keep track of the templates as you reach for them, one by one. Place all templates into a large plastic bag when you are finished with them. You'll have them all together in case you change your mind and want to recut a patch from a different fabric later.

5. Review the technique in Freezer-Paper Template Appliqué (page 7). You will be following this method exactly: ironing each template onto the right side of its fabric, marking around the edge, removing the paper, cutting it out ¼″ beyond the marked line, ironing under the edge to be appliquéd, pinning the piece in place, and machine sewing the appliquéd edge with monofilament thread in a short narrow zigzag stitch. (I set my stitch at 2.5mm wide and 1.5mm long, but your machine may be different.)

6. Appliqué pieces 1–57 into place, leaving the area marked "center piece" open. Refer to the pattern for areas where you might want to first combine patches and then appliqué them as a single unit. An example would be patches 27 and 28.

Machine and Hand Embroidering the Seams

1. Refer to Make a Stitch Sample Cloth (page 48) to make a sample piece with the fabric that you will use in the quilt, layered over some muslin that has been interfaced. You will want to try out machine stitch selections, threads, and settings here before you commit to them on the quilt.

2. Green and flower-colored threads are good choices for the bottom section of the project. Use different stitches and embroider along (or over) the seams between all the patches.

3. Choose a seam and add some simple hand embroidery stitches to it in a thread that is of similar weight. Let your imagination lead you along. You may also wish to leave some seams as they are, with no handwork.

Some of the machine-embroidered seams have added handwork and some do not.

4. Repeat the same process for the sky section, sampling threads and stitches before stitching them into the block. If your machine has it, the outline star stitch is perfect for painting. Refer to Adding Fabric Paint (page 47) to see how to paint and augment machine embroidery stitches.

5. Once the seams are completed, it is time to hang the moon and the stars. Except for the 2 circles around the moon and the Big Dipper, all the beading is random and spontaneous. Perhaps you have some constellations of your own you would like to add. Just remember to keep the beading 1″ in from the edge of the block.

Machine-embroidered and hand-painted seams, plus rich hand beading, make for a starry night showing the Big Dipper.

Making the Center Scene

Study the photo to get a sense of how this scene fits together, appliquéd from background to foreground. The sky and hills are sewn down first. Next the walkway and large shrub behind the house are added, with the house, tree, and remaining shrubs following, in that order. Finally, a few French knots are sprinkled across the base of the house.

START WITH THE SKY AND HILLS

1. Locate the *My Washougal Dream* home scene pattern on the pullout page. Trace the pattern onto the 16″ × 16″ piece of muslin as you did earlier. Fuse interfacing to the back of the muslin as before.

2. The pattern does not give you the sky and hill shapes, so use the photo as a guide to draw out your own shapes onto the muslin. Make the shapes cover the muslin, and later they will be trimmed to size.

3. Trace the hill and sky shapes on the dull side of the freezer paper. Cut out the shapes and iron them onto the blue sky and green hill fabrics. Trace around the templates, remove the paper, and cut out the shapes, leaving a ¼″ margin all the way around.

> **Note**
> If you feel comfortable doing so, you can simply free cut the sky and hill shapes based on the lines on the muslin. Just remember to include extra fabric for the seam allowances.

4. Lay the sky shape in place first. Then iron under the top edge of the first hill shape and pin it in place over the bottom edge of the sky shape.

5. Proceed as in Step 4 until all the hills are pinned into place.

6. Appliqué the hills with a clear monofilament thread in a zigzag stitch as before.

7. Outline the edges of the hills with a narrow line of machine embroidery.

Detail of center scene

ADD THE LANDSCAPING, HOUSE, AND TREE

Now that the muslin foundation is covered with sky and hills, plan to nestle the house, tree, and landscaping toward the left side on the hills. Refer to the quilt photo for placement.

1. Locate the *My Washougal Dream* appliqué house, tree, and landscaping patterns on the pullout sheet. Trace and label all the pattern pieces on the dull side of the freezer paper, paying attention to the dotted lines. These lines show where overlapping occurs as you build the scene. Cut out the templates, but mark them so you know where the overlaps will be. Save the leaf 1 and leaf 2 templates to use later.

2. Iron the templates onto your chosen fabrics. Do not cut them out yet.

3. Following the manufacturer's instructions, iron fusible web to the backs of the fabrics with the freezer-paper templates on them. Remove any paper backing from the web.

4. When you cut these pieces, do not cut a ¼" seam allowance, but where there are dotted lines, add an extra ⅛" to allow for overlap. With sharp scissors, carefully cut the templates on their solid lines (you will be cutting through both the fabric and the freezer paper at the same time).

5. Landscape pieces L1, L2, and L3 must go down first because they overlap each other, and then add L4 because it is "behind" the house. Then, slowly and carefully, fuse the appliqué house pieces into place, in numerical order, using the drawing as a guide. After the house is built, "plant" the tree, and finally finish with the rest of the landscaping, all in numerical order.

6. Once the scene is all fused into place, go over all the edges with a clear monofilament thread and a narrower zigzag than before (I set my machine to 2.0mm wide and 1.5mm long).

7. Add hand-embroidered outlines using 2 strands of floss around the doorway, roof, and walls. Sprinkle some French knots around the base of the house.

8. Hand embroider some wildflowers in the foreground on a hill. I used the fly stitch (page 33) and simple straight stitches in machine thread … but use your own imagination here!

ADD AND QUILT THE CENTER SCENE

1. Trim the scene to fit its space on the large block, overlapping the edges of the patches surrounding it by ¼".

2. Pin the scene into place and then appliqué the raw edge with a clear monofilament thread, using the wider zigzag that you used earlier (I set my machine back to a 2.5mm width and 1.5mm length).

3. Spray the 16" × 16" piece of batting. On the back of the large block, smooth the batting into place behind the center scene area.

4. Quilt the sky and along the edges of the hill shapes. Use a sky-colored thread for the sky and clear monofilament thread for the hills. I believe the house, tree, and landscaping are so small that they do not require quilting, but the larger hill shapes do or they will be too puffy.

5. Trim off any excess batting from the back.

FRAME THE SCENE

1. Pin the rickrack around the top of the scene and appliqué into place.

2. Pin the jacquard trim around the bottom of the scene and appliqué into place.

3. Machine baste along the center of the 60" length of 12mm green silk ribbon with a basting stitch on the sewing machine. Refer to Embellishing Trim and Premade Flowers (page 49). Pull the basting thread to tightly gather the ribbon. Pin gathered ribbon into place alongside the rickrack, and zigzag into place down the center of the ribbon.

4. Hand embroider an outline stitch along the top of the jacquard trim.

5. Use the leaf templates that you cut earlier to cut out 8 pairs of leaf 1 and leaf 2 from the green wool. Pin in place as shown in the photo and attach with a single row of straight machine stitching down each center.

6. Add a bead to the center of each pair of leaves.

7. Attach some small cloth flowers to the top of the gathered ribbon portion of the frame with some French knots in their centers.

Complete the Embellishment

1. Iron fusible web to the back of some garden print and green scraps.

2. Freehand, cut a nice assortment of flowers and leaves.

3. Play with the arrangement of the flowers and leaves over the garden section of the block. (Some of them may wish to "grow" and become part the frame of the center scene as well.) When you like the arrangement, iron them into place.

4. Machine appliqué the raw edges of all the flowers and leaves with clear thread in a zigzag. (My stitch was set at 2.5mm wide and 1.5mm long.)

5. Pin and appliqué the lacelike trim along the bottom of the garden scene.

6. Use the pink 13mm silk ribbon to make 9 flowers of 5 petals each along the length of the trim. Refer to Silk Ribbon Embroidery (page 39). Sew a large bead into the center of each flower.

7. Add the machine-embroidered butterfly motif if desired.

8. Finally, disassemble the premade cloth flowers so that you have single blooms. Layer them or use them individually, scattering them across the surface of the garden area, attaching them with French knots or beads in their centers. Refer to Adding Beadwork (page 47).

A detail of the completed garden section. Also shown are the embroidered hill, the wool leaves along the frame, and appliquéd flowers forming part of the frame around the central scene.

Finishing

1. Cut a 24″ × 24″ square of the backing fabric. Place it face down on a large cutting mat.

2. Layer a 24″ × 24″ square of light-weight batting over the backing fabric.

3. Center the finished quilt block, face up, over the batting.

4. Use a large ruler to mark the lines where you will trim through all 3 layers at once. Make sure that the walls of the house are perfectly vertical before you draw the trimming lines.

5. Carefully trim through the layers with a rotary cutter. (At this point my quilt was 20½″ × 18½″. Of course, yours may be different.)

6. Without moving the trimmed sandwich, pin the layers together all around the perimeter of the quilt, at 2″ intervals. You do not want the layers to shift.

7. Slowly machine stitch around the perimeter, ⅛″ from the edges, removing pins as you sew.

8. For the facing, follow the instructions in French Facing (page 30). From the backing fabric, cut border strips 3½″ wide and squares 7″ × 7″.

Resources

Suppliers

River Silks www.riversilks.com
Our favorite silk ribbon

Aurifil www.aurifil.com
Machine embroidery thread

Sulky of America www.sulky.com
Machine embroidery thread

Vicki Day Designs www.roberge-day.com
Hand-dyed silk ribbon, silks, velvets, wools, laces, and trims. See the Ode to the Amish *and* Color Block Fans *quilts for Vicki's striking colors.*

Renaissance Ribbons www.renaissanceribbons.com
Trims and ribbon

Simplicity Creative Group www.simplicity.com
Trims and ribbon

M&S Schmalberg www.customfabricflowers.com
Fabric flowers in For Love of Asia *and* My Washougal Dream

Handi Quilter www.handiquilter.com
Allie loved using the Sweet Sixteen to quilt all her projects.

AccuQuilt www.accuquilt.com
GO! Fabric Cutter, 6½" square die and 3" strip die

Brewer Sewing Supplies www.brewersewing.com
Golden Threads Quilting Paper

The Pink Bunny www.valeriebothell.com
All your crazy-quilt supply needs

For Inspiration

The Quilt Index www.quiltindex.org
A free online resource with the largest collection of documented quilts in the world. You can browse more than 50,000 quilts in these categories: Historical Collection, Time Period, Style/Techniques, Pattern, Purpose/Function, Location. There are hundreds of crazy quilts for you to discover!

International Quilt Study Center & Museum, University of Nebraska–Lincoln www.quiltstudy.org
The museum houses the largest publicly held quilt collection in the world. Its website provides information about quilts, the museum, the University of Nebraska's academic program in quilt studies, and other activities of the center.

About the Authors

Photo: Judith Baker Montano

Allie Aller has been reveling in quilting, fabric, and thread for decades, focusing intently on crazy quilting since 1999. She is the author of *Allie Aller's Crazy Quilting: Modern Piecing & Embellishing Techniques for Joyful Stitching* from C&T Publishing.

She lives in the country at the mouth of the beautiful Columbia Gorge in Washington State with her gardening husband of 33 years. They have 2 awesome grown sons and a quilting daughter-in-law!

Visit her blog at www.alliesinstitches.blogspot.com.

Also by Allie Aller:

Valerie Bothell has been happily teaching crazy quilting from her home in Wichita, Kansas, for the last 17 years. She has hosted the Victorian Stitchery Retreat for the past 7 years in her hometown. Traveling and teaching is very rewarding to her, and she always looks forward to every opportunity to share her love of crazy quilting. She has been married 20 years and has 4 very handsome sons.

You may visit her website at www.valeriebothell.com.

Great Titles and Products
from C&T PUBLISHING *and* stashBOOKS.

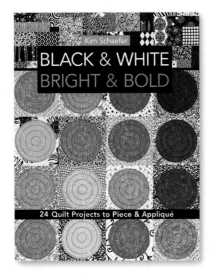

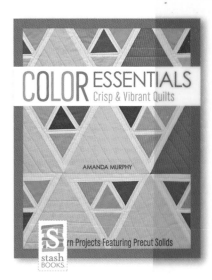

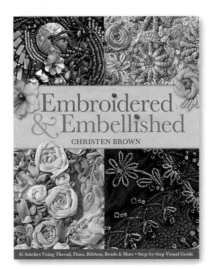

Available at your local retailer or **www.ctpub.com** *or* **800-284-1114**

For a list of other fine books from C&T Publishing, visit our website
to view our catalog online.

C&T PUBLISHING, INC.
P.O. Box 1456
Lafayette, CA 94549   Email: ctinfo@ctpub.com
800-284-1114   Website: www.ctpub.com

C&T Publishing's professional photography services are now available to
the public. Visit us at www.ctmediaservices.com.

Tips and Techniques can be found at www.ctpub.com > Consumer
Resources > Quiltmaking Basics: Tips & Techniques for Quiltmaking & More

For quilting supplies:

COTTON PATCH
1025 Brown Ave.
Lafayette, CA 94549
Store: 925-284-1177   Email: CottonPa@aol.com
Mail order: 925-283-7883   Website: www.quiltusa.com

Note: Fabrics shown may not be currently available, as fabric
manufacturers keep most fabrics in print for only a short time.